GET OUTSIDE

‹‹‹‹‹‹‹‹‹‹‹‹‹‹‹‹‹‹‹‹‹‹‹‹‹

Kids Can Press acknowledges the financial support of the
Government of Ontario, through the BPIDP, for our
publishing activity.

Published in Canada by
Kids Can Press Ltd.
25 Dockside Drive
Toronto, ON M5A 0B5

Published in the U.S. by
Kids Can Press Ltd.
2250 Military Road
Tonawanda, NY 14150

www.kidscanpress.com

This edition edited by Samantha Swenson
Original editions edited by Laurie Wark and Trudee Romanek
Interior designed by Karen Powers and Blair Kerrigan/Glyphics
Cover designed by Marie Bartholomew

This book is limp sewn with a drawn-on cover.

Manufactured in Louiseville,
QC, Canada, in 11/2011 by
Transcontinental Printing

CM PA 12 0 9 8 7 6 5 4 3 2 1

Library and Archives Canada Cataloguing in Publication

Drake, Jane
    Get outside : The kids guide to fun in the great outdoors /
by Jane Drake and Ann Love ; illustrated by Heather Collins.

Includes index.
ISBN 978-1-55453-802-7

1. Outdoor recreation — Juvenile literature. 2. Outdoor games
— Juvenile literature. I. Love, Ann II. Collins, Heather III.
Title.

GV191.62.D72 2012   j796.083   C2011-904885-X

Kids Can Press is a Corus™ Entertainment company

GET OUTSIDE

THE KIDS GUIDE TO FUN IN THE GREAT OUTDOORS

WRITTEN BY

JANE DRAKE & ANN LOVE

ILLUSTRATED BY

HEATHER COLLINS

KIDS CAN PRESS

CONTENTS

FALL

WINTER

❋ SPRING ❋

The winter is over, and warmer weather is finally arriving. Spring is the perfect time to get outside with your friends — fly a kite, play some goofy golf or break out those baseball mitts that have been waiting since fall! It's also a great time to welcome back the local wildlife by building a bat hangout or birdhouse. Spring rains have you trapped inside? Learn some new card games you can play with your friends. Springtime will be fun time with these great activities!

BUILD A BIRDHOUSE

Just as different kinds of birds look different, they like different nests and nesting sites. Here's an easy birdhouse to make that will suit a bluebird, a tree swallow, a flicker or a house wren.

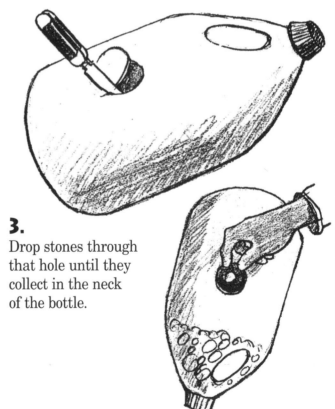

You'll need:
a large plastic vinegar or bleach bottle (half size for wrens)
muddy water
gravel
a sharp knife
small stones
a hammer and nail
coarse sandpaper
brown exterior house-type paint and a paintbrush
wire to tie the house to a tree or post

2.

Turn the bottle upside down and ask an adult to help you cut a circular hole on one side with your knife. The hole should be well above the neck of the bottle. The hole size determines the kind of birds you'll attract (see the list on the next page).

1.

Wash out the plastic bottle thoroughly. Make a mixture of muddy water and gravel. Swirl it around inside the bottle and pour it out again. This will take away the chemical smell and leave a rougher, more natural surface on the inside.

3.

Drop stones through that hole until they collect in the neck of the bottle.

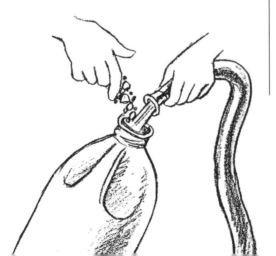

4.
Make two small air holes on the sides above the entrance hole.

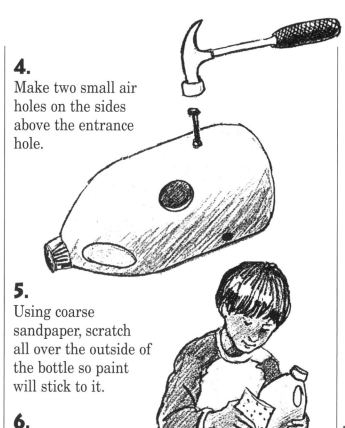

5.
Using coarse sandpaper, scratch all over the outside of the bottle so paint will stick to it.

6.
Paint the outside of the birdhouse a light brown color to make it look like wood. Don't paint the neck of the bottle. While the paint is still wet, carry the bottle to a wooded area and roll it in leaf and twig litter until some has stuck to the paint.

7.
When the paint is dry, run wire through the air holes and out the back. Strap the house to a tree or post and at a height favored by your chosen bird (see the list below). Remove the cap for drainage.

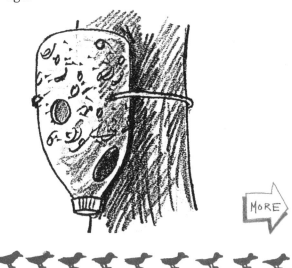

MORE →

BIRDHOUSE FACTS

Kind of Bird	Hole Size	Nesting Location
bluebird	4 cm (1 1/2 in.)	about 1.5 m (5 ft.) off the ground on a post in open country about 10 m (32 ft.) from a tree
tree swallow	5 cm (2 in.)	a little higher off the ground than for a bluebird and near a pond
flicker	7–8 cm (3 in.)	about 5 m (16 ft.) up a tree trunk on a woodland edge
house wren	3 cm (1 in.)	on the trunk of a thick shrub about 1 m (3 ft.) off the ground; house wrens like two houses, one for the young, one for extra nesting materials

PURPLE MARTIN APARTMENT HOUSE

With the help of an adult, you can construct a purple martin apartment house.

1.

Make six or more plastic-bottle birdhouses as described on page 8, except work with each plastic bottle right-side-up, lid screwed on.

2.

Cut a 5 cm (2 in.) entrance hole for each unit.

3.

Don't drop stones into the neck. Instead, make a few small nail holes in the bottom of the bottle so any rainwater will drain away.

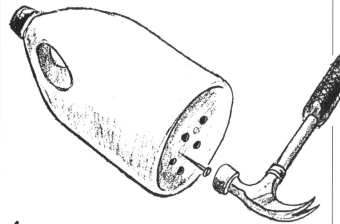

4.

Hang the houses in threes along a wooden bar using wire.

5.

With your adult helper, nail the wooden bars on top of a pole at a height of 3 m (10 ft.) or up to 7m (23 ft.).

Purple martins like an open yard away from trees and buildings but near a pond or lake so they can feast on insects such as mosquitoes. Set up your martin apartment early in the spring and you may have a busy colony of families by summer. Pioneers believed that if they sprinkled broken eggshells under a martin house, it was more likely to be chosen as a colony house. Why not try it, too?

NATURE BREAK

In 1884, a man actually counted the number of times adult martins in a colony visited their young with food in one day. He counted 3277 visits. When purple martins move into your colony, try sitting outside in the evening to see if you get bothered by mosquitoes. People who have martins near their homes often say they are never bothered by bugs — the martins have eaten them all.

BUILD A BAT HANGOUT

One bat can eat 500 mosquitoes an hour on a spring or summer's night. Why not make a bat box so you can make use of this remarkable and cheap insect-control service?

You'll need:
a hand saw
a rough, unplaned untreated plank of wood at least 2 cm (3/4 in.) thick and 15 cm (6 in.) wide
a pencil
4 smaller strips of wood, each about 2 cm (3/4 in.) wide and 15 cm (6 in.) long
white carpenter's glue
a hammer
nails or screws and screwdriver
tacks
scrap of tarpaper (a dark green plastic garbage bag will also work)

1.

Ask an adult to help you saw a piece of plank about 25 cm (10 in.) long for the backboard.

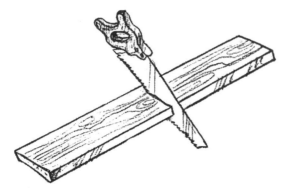

2.

Saw another piece at least 15 cm (6 in.) long for a frontboard. Lay the frontboard on the backboard a few centimetres (1 in.) down from the top and draw a pencil line on the backboard all around where the front sits.

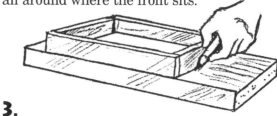

3.

Lay your smaller strips of wood along the pencil line and cut them with the saw so they fit neatly right around. Trim the floor strip about 4 cm (1 1/2 in.) shorter than the length of the bottom and angle it upward to make an entrance.

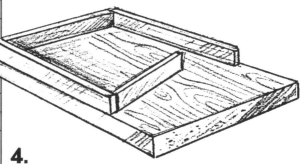

4.

Glue the side and top strips on edge onto the backboard. Nail or screw them in place. Screw on the bottom strip, but leave it loose so that it can be tilted to clean out the bat box once a year.

5.

Smear glue along the edge of the top and side strips and lay on the frontboard. Then, nail or screw the frontboard down.

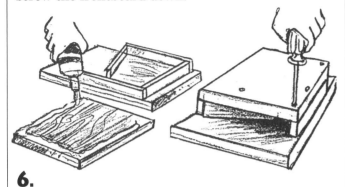

6.

Tack tarpaper on the back of the backboard, pull it over the top and tack it part way down the frontboard.

7.

Now, hang your bat box. Choose a spot sheltered from the wind, on an outside wall or on a tree but away from branches, and facing southwest or southeast so that the inside will get warm in the sun. Your box is best sited near a meadow or pond where night-time mosquito hunting is good. Nail the backboard top and bottom so the entrance is at least 5 m (16 ft.) off the ground.

BAT FACTS

- Bats may move into your bat box soon after it's hung — and will even go house-hunting as early as April. Leave your box up over the winter.
- In summer, mother bats like their nest to be toasty warm — 26 to 32°C (80 to 90°F) if possible. Males choose cooler hangouts away from the young.
- Bats roost by day and fly off to feed at night. Watch your box at dusk to see bats take off.
- Bats are fussy about personal hygiene. They lick their fur, scratch themselves and wipe their faces. They are particularly fussy about keeping their wings clean. Bat poop, called guano, is a great fertilizer for your garden. It will collect under the bat box.
- Most northern bats eat only insects. In some parts of the world, bats eat pollen and are important pollinators of fruits. Blood-sucking vampire bats are tropical.
- Bats will leave their nesting spots by September to look for warmer winter hang-outs in hollow trees, caves and the attics of old buildings. They hibernate over winter.

SWAMP THINGS

Where can you find an insect that will pierce the skin of a victim three times its size, turn all the victim's insides into a soup and suck them out? In your local swamp — that's where. Water tigers are just one of many fascinating mini-beasts that live in swamp water. Here's how you can take a closer look at some of these strange creations.

You'll need:
a medium-sized pail
a small plastic container (such as a margarine or yogurt tub)
a large glass bottle (such as a huge pickle jar)
a white sheet or counter top

1.
Carry the pail and plastic container to the nearest still-water pond or swamp. Wear rubber boots and take along an adult and a friend.

2.
Stand on a firm spot at the edge of the swamp and dip into the water with your plastic container. When you catch a swamp thing — something small like a wiggling bug or plant — pour it into the pail. Don't pour in muddy water.

3.
When your pail is as full as you can carry, it's time to go home.

4.
Pour the swamp water into your jar and set it on a white sheet or countertop away from the direct sun. Do not cover the jar. (If you have leftover swamp water in the pail, return it to the swamp.)

5.
Have a look every day at your jar. Strange new creatures will suddenly appear when tiny eggs in the rich swamp water hatch. Familiar creatures will drastically change or fall prey to hungry predators. Some will lay eggs you cannot see and then the adults will disappear. You are watching the daily dramas of the swamp.

6.
Add a little fresh swamp water every morning so the creatures will always have a healthy food supply.

7.
After you watch the swamp things for a few days, return the creatures and their water to their natural home in the swamp. Lower your pail right into the swamp and pour out the water slowly.

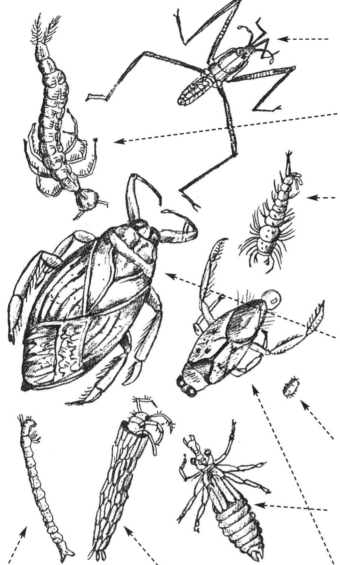

Water striders live on the surface of the swamp and never sink.

The **water tiger** injects into its prey a juice that digests the victim's body before it's eaten.

Mosquito larvae use a breathing tube like a snorkel they stick through the surface of the water. Watch for a mosquito to hatch out of the water, dry its wings and fly away.

The female **giant water bug** cements her eggs onto the back of the male, who then carries them around until they hatch.

That tiny red dot with eight whirling legs is likely a **water mite**.

A **dragonfly nymph** jerks along the bottom because it moves by squirting water out of its behind.

If you see two black eyes on what looks like a see-through body, it's probably a **phantom midge larva**. You can see the phantom midge larvae best if you hold a piece of black paper behind the jar. Like all ghosts, the phantom midge larva is most active at night.

Do you see a bunch of twigs swimming together? It's probably the house of a **caddisfly larva**. Look carefully and a creature will stick its head out one end to grab another piece of construction material. Some varieties will use bits of plant, pebbles or even tiny snails.

A **backswimmer** is a wild scuba diver. That silvery flash at the end of its body is an air bubble, a reserve tank for use until it can get back to the surface. When it's time for a refill, the backswimmer stops paddling and the bubble floats the bug to the surface.

EC👁WATCH

It's best not to collect bigger swamp things such as frogs, toads, salamanders or turtles. They don't survive well in a pail or a bottle and are easily injured by people's hands. Don't disturb or collect their eggs either because when they're removed from their natural home, few ever hatch.

Unfortunately, many of our wetlands, such as swamps and marshes, were used as dumps or were drained in past years. Some of the larger swamp creatures became rare. Most people are more careful with wetlands now because they realize wetlands are important storage areas for freshwater as well as breeding grounds for many kinds of wildlife.

If you have a wetland near your home, you have a special place. Make sure everybody treats it with care!

ANIMAL CLUES

You don't have to see an animal to know that it has visited your yard or local park. Animals leave behind clues that clearly say "I've been here." So be a detective and find the clues that tell you who has visited.

RACCOON

Overturned garbage, pilfered compost, crayfish remains on the beach all indicate that the masked bandit has dined nearby. Raccoon paw prints look like tiny human hands.

SKUNK

If your nose doesn't tell you, your lawn will. Holes and rolled-up grass show where the skunk's sharp claws have scrounged a meal of grubs and insects.

DEER

Look for flattened grass in meadows or woodland clearings. You've had a sleepover guest. Check under apple trees, too — deer love apples for breakfast.

SQUIRREL

The log pile is a good hide out for a squirrel, mouse or chipmunk. If you find pine cones that have been eaten clean, you have a tenant.

PLASTER-CAST ANIMAL TRACKS

You can make a "negative" impression plaster cast of a bird or animal track. They make pretty impressive doorstops or paperweights.

You'll need:

heavy cardboard 5 cm x 20 cm (2 in. x 8 in.)
a paper clip
a margarine tub
Polyfix or other wall plaster
a stick

1.
Find a clear animal or bird track in mud or sand.

2.
Form the cardboard into a circle, securing it with a paper clip. Place the cardboard around the track and push it gently into the soil or sand.

3.
Pour enough water into the margarine tub to half fill the cardboard mould. Add the plaster a little at a time, stirring with a stick until smooth. The mixture should be as thick as pancake batter. It should pour but not be too runny.

4.
Pour the plaster into the mould.

5.
Let it set for several hours until it's very hard. Drying time will depend on how thick your cast is and the dampness in the air.

6.
Remove the plaster cast from the ground, removing the cardboard mould. Dust off any loose dirt.

7.
You can paint the track or leave it white.

GOOFY GOLF

The makings of a miniature golf course are hiding in your home. Scavenge through the shed, kitchen cupboards and toy box, and you'll find prefabricated obstacles. Then the only other things you'll need are a golf ball and a putter for each player. If you don't have putters, use hockey sticks, croquet mallets or umbrellas instead.

GETTING READY

- Ask an adult to help you set up your golf course. Make flags from straightened coat hangers and triangles of paper.

- Choose an outdoor play area to set up your course — a lawn, park or playing field will do. You don't need a large area. Fairways can zigzag back and forth across one another. It's easier to putt on grass that is short. Make use of what your play area has to offer — shots can go under a tree, over a mound of earth, along a smooth path and so on.

- Establish a starting line and lay out a continuous course of nine "holes" with one obstacle and one flag per hole. Use the flag plus stones or wooden sticks as pegs to hold any wobbly obstacles in place.

AN EAVES-TROUGH-PIPE ELBOW

BUILDING-BLOCK GATES

A NATURAL HOLE

A TIN CAN OPEN AT BOTH ENDS

1 M (3 FT.) OF DRYER HOSE

START

A WOODEN RAMP

8

6

9

FINISH

A TIN CAN AND PINWHEEL

FOUR CROQUET HOOPS

4

3

TWO PIECES OF THICK WOOD

PLAYING THE GAME

Choose one player to go first. She shoots her golf ball from the starting line to the first hole and through it, keeping track of the number of shots she takes. All other players do the same. Don't pick up your golf ball between holes, just putt to the next obstacle. Continue until each player has completed the course. The player with the lowest score is the winner.

Store the parts of the game in a box or return borrowed obstacles at the end of the game.

OTHER GOOFY OBSTACLES

a fruit basket

1 m (3 ft.) of plastic drainage pipe

a wooden bridge

an ice cream pail

a shoe box

a large cardboard poster tube

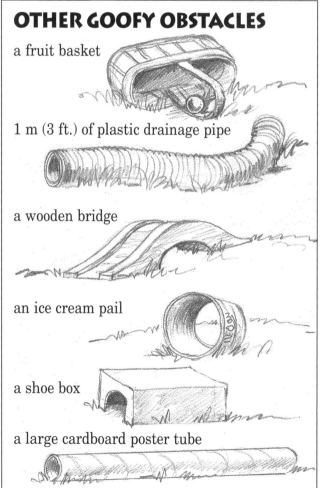

19

COOPERATIVE GAMES

Get the whole gang working together for a change. Set up a challenge that will not be successful unless everyone helps one another to complete it.

◆ ◆ ◆ ◆ ◆ ◆ ◆ ◆ ◆ ◆ ◆ ◆ ◆

LIFE RAFT

This game is played on land, but you pretend the ground is shark-infested water. For a group of ten, you'll need a beach towel. If you have more friends who want to join in, grab an old tablecloth or sheet.

PLAYING THE GAME

1.
Lay the towel flat on the ground.

2.
Challenge your friends to huddle on the cloth so that no one touches the ground beyond. Hold that position for a count of ten.

3.
When you've accomplished that feat, fold the towel in half and try again.

4.
See how small a space you can all huddle on — with no one getting a toe nibbled off by the circling sharks.

S P I D E R   W E B

1.

Find a place where two trees grow about 3 m (9 ft.) apart. Take a full ball of nylon rope and tie one end to one tree, about 30 cm (1 ft.) up the trunk. Pull the rope up the side of the tree, and loop it around the same trunk and knot it again at 1 m (3 ft.) and 2 m (6 ft.) for strength.

2.

Pull the rope across to the other tree, loop and tie around that trunk at about 2 m (6 ft.), 1 m (3 ft.) and 30 cm (1 ft.), too. Complete the rectangle by returning the rope to the first knot.

3.

Now, weave a web between the two trees. Leave some spaces about 65 cm (2 ft.) square in the mesh. If you have any little decorative bells on threads or elastics, dangle them onto some of the strands of the web.

4.

Challenge the whole group to get through the web without touching the strands or trees so as not to awaken the people-eating spider. Only one person in the group is allowed to crawl under the web.

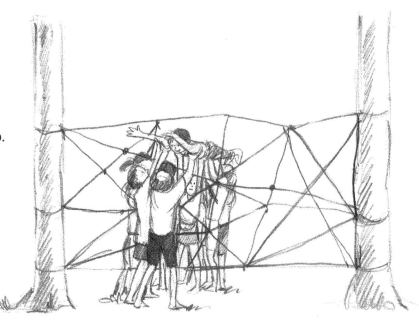

JUGGLE BUBBLES

Touch a bubble and it bursts, right? Try making the bubble mixture below, and with careful handling, you can make bubbles that last a little longer. It's best to do this outside, unless you like mopping floors.

BUBBLE SOLUTION

You'll need:
50 mL (¼ c.) of dish detergent
175 mL (¾ c.) of cold water
5 drops of glycerin

Why do bubbles burst? It's because the water in the bubble solution evaporates in the air and the bubbles dry out. Pop. The glycerin in this mixture slows down this process, helping the bubbles last longer.

BUBBLE BLOWERS

Make your own bubble blowers using wire and pliers. A thin coat hanger easily bends into a small circle with a handle. Make other shapes — diamonds, figure eights and squares. Your cutlery drawer may contain ready-made bubble blowers. Try a potato masher, plastic funnel, slatted spoon, apple corer, plastic straw...

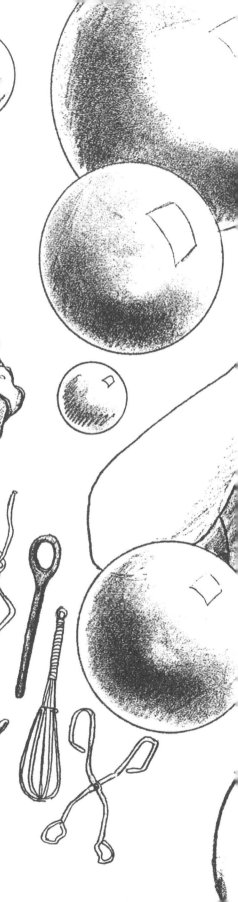

JUGGLE YOUR BUBBLES

Pull on a pair of cotton or woollen mittens or gloves. Blow a bubble and, with a cupped palm, bounce your bubble into the air. See how many times you can touch it before it goes poof.

23

FLY A KITE

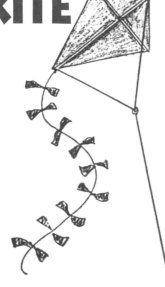

There's nothing like the feel of a kite pulling up and away from your grip on a windy day. Why not make a kite so you're ready when steady breezes blow?

You'll need:
a felt-tip pen
a tape measure
2 straight sticks or dowelling, about 5 mm (1/4 in.) thick and about 70 cm (28 in.) long
1 m (3 ft.) fishing line
40 m (130 ft.) strong, thin (1 mm) nylon cord
4 straight pins
a piece of light cotton about 80 cm x 80 cm (32 in. x 32 in.)
scissors
white glue
colored tissue paper
a metal pop can opening tab
a flat wooden stick about 15 cm (6 in.) long

1.
Start by making the frame. With a felt-tip pen, mark a point 20 cm (8 in.) from the end of one stick and then mark a point 35 cm (14 in.) from the end of the other stick. Form a cross with the two sticks so they meet at your two marks. Wind the fishing line crosswise around the joint and knot securely.

2.
Cut off about 4.5 m (15 ft.) of the nylon cord. Pin one end of the cord into the bottom tip of the frame. Stretch the cord around the frame and pin it at the other three tips. Bring it back to the bottom and secure it with the first pin. Leave the remaining cord attached to form the kite tail.

3.
Lay the completed frame on the cotton fabric and cut out the kite shape, leaving an extra 2 cm (3/4 in.) all around. Snip little "V's" out of each point of the shape.

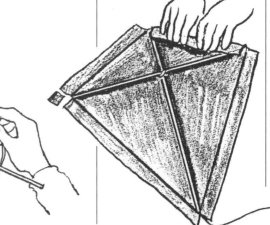

4.
Spread glue over the 2 cm (3/4 in.) margin you left and then fold and press it back over the frame.

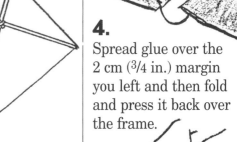

24

5.

To finish off the tail, cut the tissue paper into strips about 30 cm x 15 cm (12 in. x 6 in.) long. Fold the strips in half lengthwise. Tie the middle of the strips to the tail string of the kite, spacing them about 15 cm (6 in.) apart.

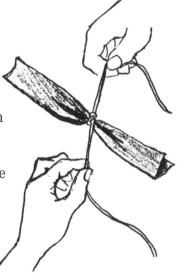

6.

Now it's time to string the kite. Cut 120 cm (47 in.) of cord, fold it in half, push the loop end through the pop-can ring and then slip the loose ends back through the loop. Open up the cord and tie one end to the top of the kite spine and the other to the bottom.

7.

Tie one end of the remaining nylon cord to the flat wooden stick. Wind the cord around and around until you come to the other end. Tie that to the pop-can ring. Now you have your kite attached to its line and you're ready to fly it.

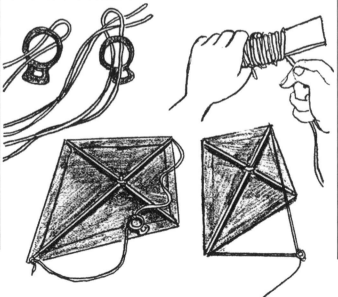

TIPS FOR SUCCESSFUL KITE FLYING

Choose a clear day with a steady wind to try out your kite. Gusty days are hard for beginners. Stand in a place where the wind will blow your kite away from any electrical wires or kite-eating trees.

Let out a few metres (several feet) of the kite line. Ask a friend to toss the kite high in the air while you run the other way, into the wind, letting out line as you go.

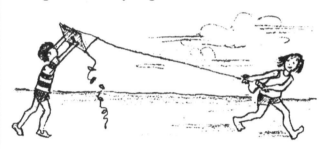

If the kite keeps nosediving, add cord to lengthen the tail. If it keeps falling backward, shorten the tail.

Remember, never fly kites near power lines because you can get electrocuted.

NEVER FLY A KITE DURING A THUNDER-STORM!

CRAZY KITES

Before you glue on your swatch of light cotton fabric, try painting crazy animal faces or insect bodies on it. Your kite could look like a snarling cat, a lovely butterfly or a monster mosquito.

500 UP

It's a perfect day for baseball but you don't have enough players for a game. Why not play 500 Up? You'll still get that warm, timeless baseball feeling — and practice your skills at the same time. You'll need two or more players, a bat, a ball and baseball gloves if you have them, and a large open area so you can hit the ball safely. If you don't have a baseball and bat, a tennis ball and racket will do.

PLAYING THE GAME

One player starts as the batter and everyone else is a fielder. The batter stands at one end of the field, throws the ball up in the air and hits it out into the field.

All fielders try to catch the ball. The fielder who does scores a certain number of points depending on the type of catch. Any fielder who tries for the ball and fumbles it loses points. When a player tallies up 500 points, that player becomes the new batter and the previous batter takes a place in the field. The game goes on until you run out of energy.

26

SCORING

A fielder who catches	A fielder who fumbles and misses
a fly earns 100 points	a fly loses 100 points
a ball that bounces once earns 75 points	a ball that bounces once loses 75 points
a ball that bounces twice earns 50 points	a ball that bounces twice loses 50 points
a ball that bounces more than twice (a grounder) earns 25 points	a ball that bounces more than twice (a grounder) loses 25 points

LEMON SODA

If you're feeling hot and thirsty after your baseball playing, try this on for size! You'll be cooled off in no time.

You'll need:
juice of one lemon or orange
glass of water
2 ice cubes
5 mL (1 tsp.) sugar
5 mL (1 tsp.) baking soda

1.
Mix the freshly squeezed juice with water and sugar in a glass.

2.
Add 2 ice cubes and the baking soda.

3.
Stir in some bubbles and drink up. Ahhhhh, now that's refreshing.

27

STONE TOSS GAMES

A walk along a pebbly beach with a parent or a friend is a relaxing way to end a spring day. You may notice twists of rope, driftwood shapes, bits of animal bone — all weathered remains that have a story to tell.

Here are some objects to pick up on the beach and games to play with them as you walk along.

BULLFROG GLUG

Look for a stone about the size and shape of a plum. It should be heavy and sit easily in the curled palm of your hand.

Check around you. Make sure no one is close by or out in the water. Throw the stone so it arcs high in the air and then falls straight down into the water.

If you make a good throw, and you have a good stone, when it enters the water it will make the glugging sound of a bullfrog croak.

S K I P P I N G   S T O N E S

If the water is calm, look along the beach for thin, flat, circular stones, about as a big around as potato chips. Collect a few in your pocket.

Check to make sure no one is in front of you, on either side or in the water. It's okay for friends to stand behind you. Hold a stone so its widest part is held in the U-shaped arc between your index finger and your thumb and its flattest side faces down. Stand so your body is sideways to the water. Bend your knees and hold the stone low, almost level with the water. Swing your arm behind your body and then forward, straightening your index finger as your hand passes your waist.

The stone will run along your finger and then spin toward the water, with the flat side still facing down. When it hits the water surface, it should skip up, fall again, skip up — over and over, until it finally sinks.

How many times can you make it skip? Set a family record, or is that a "rockord"?

FOSSIL WATCH

Some of the stones you pick up may have regular patterns on them, like tiny tire treads or delicate swirls. You may have found a fossil — plant or animal remains from millions of years ago. When the plant or animal died, by chance it was trapped immediately in mud so deep that, over the years, the mud slowly turned to stone. If you find a fossil, you may not want to skip it.

NIGHT PROWL

What goes bump outside in the night? If you really want to know, you can take a night prowl. You'll be surprised at who's making those noises out there.

You'll need:
a red bandanna or scarf
a flashlight
dark clothing (be sure to stay away from roads)
a friend or an adult

1.
Tie the red bandanna over your flashlight so when it's on, the light is still strong but glows red.

2.
Wait for a clear night and put on your dark clothes. Rub dirt on your face and hands, too, if you want to really act the part.

3.
Take a friend and tell an adult where you're going and when you'll be back. Step outside, away from the house lights, and turn on your flashlight.

4.
Stand still to get used to the dark. Look at the trees and watch how moonlight and breezes play on them. Each kind of tree moves in its own way. Maples, for instance, have a darker leaf top than underside so when a breeze passes, the whole tree ripples light and dark like running water.

5.

When you're used to the dark, walk ahead softly. Sweep the dark with your light. When you hear a sound, track it in the flashlight beam.

Here are some of the things you may see and what they likely are:

black, zigzagging shadows in the air	bats
flashes of light in the grass or bushes	fireflies
tiny glowing dots of light on the ground or in rotting logs	beetle grubs or fungus
tiny, crawling specks of white	wolf spider eyes
bright yellow eyeshine	raccoon
shining green eyeshine	bullfrog
bright white eyeshine	**dog, coyote or wolf**
dull white eyeshine	whip-poor-will
flash of white tails hopping near the ground	cottontail rabbit
bounding away above eye-level	**white-tailed deer**
white streaks waddling along the ground	skunk
a silent shadow gliding tree to tree	owl
large, close-set, orange eyeshine	bear — oops — walk away noisily, yelling and throwing things hard on the ground

NIGHT ◑WL

When you hear an owl call, stop and listen for the next round. Count the number of sounds and memorize the rhythm. When you think you've got it, repeat the call several times. The owl may come to investigate, thinking you're another owl trespassing on its territory.

Here are the sounds and rhythms of owl calls you may hear:

HOOTING:
great horned owl
  WhaWhaWha - Whooo - Whooo
  WhaWhaWhaWha - Whooo - Whooo

barred owl
  Whoo - Whoo - WhaWho - Whoohoohoohoaw
  (Who cooks, who cooks for you all)

SHRIEKING:
barn owl
  Chaaaaaaaaaaaaaaaaaaaaaaaaak
  (can hiss, too)

long-eared owl
  Waaaaaaaaaaaaaaaaaaaaaaaaaaaa
  (can be wheezy or shrill)

WAILING:
screech owl
  Oo-o-o-o-o-o-o-o-o-o-000000
  (descending and quavering like a faraway ghost)

SCAVENGER HUNT

Every scavenger hunt is a one-of-a-kind event — the fun lies in the hunting and in making up a crazy adaptation to suit your outside space. If you and a group of friends create one, together you supervise the hunt and decide on the winner. You'll need a pencil and paper, at least six friends divided into two or more teams, a bag for each team to collect things in, and a large, interesting outdoor space.

GETTING READY

- Ask an adult what places are unsafe and declare them out of bounds. Depending on where you are, unsafe areas could be across the street or near water. Homes are usually out of bounds, too.

- For an hour-long hunt, make a list of about 30 things to collect. Include some items that should be easy to find. Add some that are harder to locate or will take a little thinking. Then, include some impossible things that kids may have to invent. You can star hard-to-find items and offer a bonus point for each of them.

1 wet towel
5 smooth stones
2 horse feathers
exactly 57 of something *
4 round leaves
1 solar collector
1 dirty sock
2 bikini bottoms
1 piece of kindling
6 bear paws *
1 yummy dessert
1 dandelion flower
a fastener *

PLAYING THE GAME

At the beginning of the game, set a time limit and give each team a list of items to find and a bag. Make sure everyone knows the rules:

- all items must be found or borrowed with permission; nothing should be stolen or bought just for the game

- players must stay outdoors and in bounds

When time is up, each team presents its findings, as convincingly as possible, to the other participants. Total the points and bonus points to decide which team wins.

ABC SCAVENGER HUNT

In this quick and easy hunt, everyone can play, even the organizers. Players decide on a time limit, for example, 30 minutes. Then each player or team takes a bag and heads off to find one item that begins with each letter of the alphabet. The person or team that finds the most items in the time set, wins.

WILD SCAVENGERS

Vultures are scavengers that feed on dead and rotting animals. They soar high in the air and find their deliciously putrid meals by smelling them out. Unless you have an unusually keen sense of smell, you'll find most items in a scavenger hunt using your eyes — you'll rarely sniff one out.

DONKEY

The object of this card game is to become the president. Then it's up to the other players to topple the president from power. All you need is a full deck of cards with jokers and three or more players.

PLAYING THE FIRST ROUND

1.
Choose a dealer by cutting the deck. The person who turns over the highest card shuffles and deals out the entire deck.

2.
Players sort their hand in value order, with jokers highest, followed by 2s, aces, kings, queens, jacks, 10s and so on down to 3s.

3.
The dealer starts play by laying down a card or cards of his choice. If he has four of a kind (four 3s, for example), he starts with that. Other players follow, in a clockwise manner, playing four of a kind of a greater value than the person before them or they pass.

4.

In play:

- a joker beats any lead, including four of a kind

- two 2s beat three or four of a kind, but not a joker

- one 2 beats two of a kind or any lead lower than 2

5.

The last player who is able to follow the dealer's lead leads next with three or two of a kind, or any card of her choosing. Continue playing until a player is out of cards. She becomes the president.

6.

The player to the left of the president leads, and play continues until another player is out of cards. This person is called the vice president.

7.

The player to the left of the vice president leads next. Continue until all players are out of cards. Any players to finish after the vice president are called clerks, but the last person to get rid of his cards is called the donkey.

PLAYING THE REST OF THE GAME

1.

The president shuffles the deck. The person to her left cuts the cards. Then the president deals out the entire deck.

2.

Players sort their cards by value. Before play begins, the donkey gives his two best cards to the president and the president gives the donkey two cards of her choice, usually low cards. The lowest clerk gives the vice president her highest card and the vice president gives the clerk a card of his choice, usually the lowest. When there are three players, only the president and donkey exchange cards.

SLAPJACK

Get pumped up with this fast-paced game. Shuffle together several old decks — they don't need to be complete — and play with two or more people of any age. Just remember to slap gently. A quick hand beats a heavy one, hands down.

PLAYING THE GAME

1.
Deal out all the cards in a clockwise direction. The cards are left facedown in a pile in front of each player.

2.
All players watch like hawks as the person to the left of the dealer takes the top card from his pile and places it faceup in the center of the table.

3.
If the card turned up is a jack, everyone tries to be the first to slap the card. The person whose hand hits the jack first gets the card and adds it to the bottom of her pile.

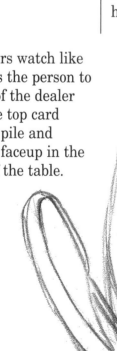

4.

If the card turned up is not a jack, the next person to the left adds a card faceup on the center pile and so on around the table. Tension mounts while players wait for the next jack and the jackpot of cards builds. The player who wins each slap gets all the cards in the pile.

5.

When a player runs out of cards, she is allowed to stay in the game, but she must be the first one to hit the next jack. If she is not, she is out.

6.

If a player makes a mistake and hits the center pile when it's not a jack, she gives the top card from her pile to the player whose card she hit.

7.

The game is over when one person has won all the cards. If this takes too long, the player with the most cards after 30 minutes wins.

WHOSE HAND HIT FIRST?

If two or more players claim to be first to the jack, check the stack of hands. Whoever's hand is on the jack at the bottom of the pile gets the jackpot.

DOMINOES

A domino tile is like two dice that have been rolled and then attached side by side to form a rectangle. In fact, that may be how dominoes were invented. Most sets are for two to four players and have 28 tiles, the highest tile being a double 6 — six dots on each end of the tile. You may, however, have a larger set that goes to double 9 or even double 12. The larger the set, the more people can play.

PLAYING DOMINOES

1.
Players place all the tiles on a flat surface facedown and shuffle them around.

2.
Each player turns up one tile, and the person whose tile has the highest number starts. The player on the left of the starter will go second, the next left third, and so on.

3.
Return the tiles to the center and reshuffle. If two people are playing, they each select seven tiles. With three or four players, each person selects five tiles. Stand the selected tiles on their sides so no one else can see them. All remaining tiles are pushed aside and may or may not be used, depending on the game.

Some tiles have a blank at one end. The blank end is wild. The player who uses one decides the value of the blank end and it keeps that value.

THE BLOCK GAME

The first player puts any tile down on the table. The second person must play a tile that has an end that matches either end of the first tile played.

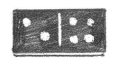

The second tile is placed matching end to matching end with the first tile in a straight line. If the second player has no matching tile to play, she loses her turn and the next person tries. The game continues until no one is able to add a tile to either end of the line.

When a player has played all her tiles, she wins. When no one can put down any more tiles and the game is blocked, the person with the lowest total number of dots on her remaining tiles wins the round. The winner adds her dot count (if she has one) to everyone else's and that total becomes her score for the round. Games are usually played to 121.

DOMINO!

T H E   D O M I N O   E F F E C T

Stand up a set of dominoes in a line. Each one is placed on its end, close enough to the next domino so that when any one is knocked over, it will knock over the one behind it. Then, tap the domino at the end of the line and watch them all topple over, one after another.

39

FIVES AND ONES

Are you lucky at dice? There are big points to be won in this game. You'll need three dice raided from other games, a pen and a piece of paper, and at least two players. The first one to 5000 wins. Here's hoping your luck holds!

SCORING

- = 50 points

- = 100 points

- three of a kind are worth the sum of the three dice multiplied by 100, for example

 x 100

= 1200 points

- If you roll 2, 3 and 4 together, you lose 100 points. There are no negative scores, so if your score was 50, your new score is 0.

= –100 points

PLAYING THE GAME

1.
Each player rolls one die. The highest roll goes first.

2.
Before you can get on the scoreboard, you must roll at least 300 points in three rolls, for example:

First roll = 50 points

Second roll = 100 points

Third roll = 150 points

Total = 300 points

3.
Once a player has reached 300, he can either put his points on the scoreboard and end his turn or throw again, trying to gain more points. If he rolls and fails, his turn is over and on his next turn he must start all over again.

4.
If a player fails to score 300 points in three rolls, the next player tries her luck.

5.

Once a player is on the board, he may roll as many times as he wants in his turn, as long as a 5, 1 or three of a kind are rolled. The player can end his turn anytime and add his points to the board. If he fails to roll a 5, 1 or three of a kind, he loses the points gained on that turn and his turn is over. Tip: it's better to quit while you're ahead.

6.

If a player rolls a 2, 3 and 4, her turn is over and she loses all the points acquired during that turn, as well as 100 points.

7.

When a player reaches 5000, the other player or players have one more turn to try to beat him.

WHAT TO LOOK FOR IN THE SPRING SKY

Once you locate the Big Dipper, you can use it to star hop and find the main constellations in the spring sky.

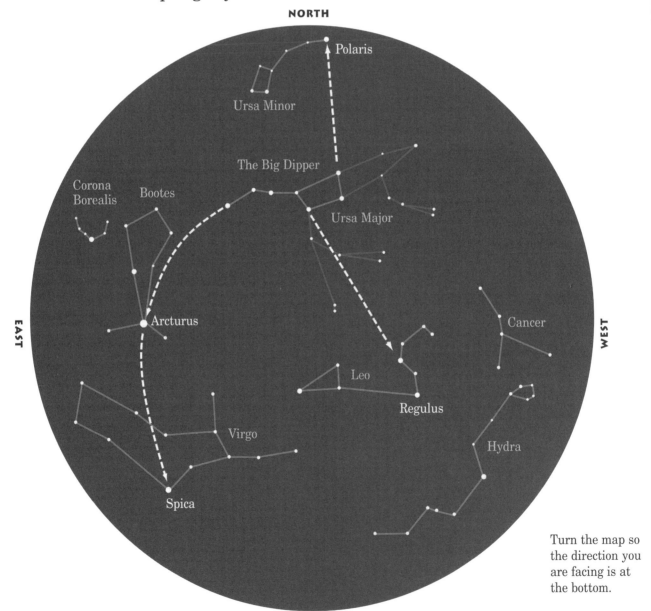

Turn the map so the direction you are facing is at the bottom.

URSA MAJOR, THE GREAT BEAR, AND URSA MINOR, THE LITTLE BEAR

Spring is the best time to find all the faint stars that make up the sky bears. The Big Dipper is a group of stars that form the Great Bear's hind end and tail. Polaris is the tip of the Little Bear's tail (see stories pages 46–47 and 132–133).

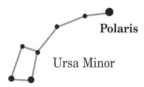

Polaris

Ursa Minor

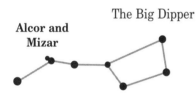

The Big Dipper

Alcor and Mizar

ALCOR AND MIZAR

Look at the star second from the end of the Big Dipper's handle. Do you see two stars instead of one? Ancient Arabs used this double star as an eye test. They said if you could see dimmer Alcor as well as brighter Mizar, you had good eyesight.

ARCTURUS

The brightest star in the spring sky, Arcturus is found by following the arc of the Big Dipper's handle. Arcturus is a giant orange-yellow star near the bottom of the constellation Bootes, the Herdsman.

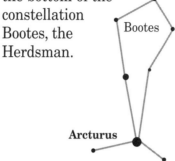

Bootes

Arcturus

CORONA BOREALIS, THE NORTHERN CROWN

By late spring, this small circlet of stars glitters east of Arcturus.

Corona Borealis

SPICA

From Arcturus, you spike south to Spica. Spica is the main star in Virgo, the Maiden and one of the brightest stars in the spring sky.

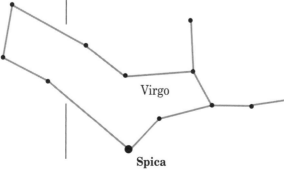

Virgo

Spica

HYDRA, THE WATER SNAKE

This constellation's tail writhes south of Spica. Look for five bright stars close together under Cancer, the Crab, to find its head. Hydra may be faint, but it's the longest and largest constellation in the spring night sky.

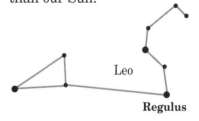

Hydra

REGULUS

At the heart of Leo, the Lion is the star Regulus, which is 150 times brighter than our Sun.

Leo

Regulus

Regulus is the dot in a group of stars that looks like a backward question mark — the head and mane of Leo, the Lion. The lion's hind end is a triangle of stars to the east of Regulus.

43

THE SPRING EQUINOX

There is one night in spring, usually March 21, when both night and day are exactly twelve hours long. On only one other day of the year does this happen — usually September 21.

An equinox is reached when the Sun crosses the celestial equator, an imaginary line across the sky directly above Earth's equator. If you were to stand on Earth's equator at noon on the equinox, you would cast no shadow. The Sun rises directly in the east and sets directly in the west at the equinox.

THE MOON AND THE EQUINOX

Because the Moon usually travels along the same path as the Sun, look for these special effects of the Moon at the spring equinox.

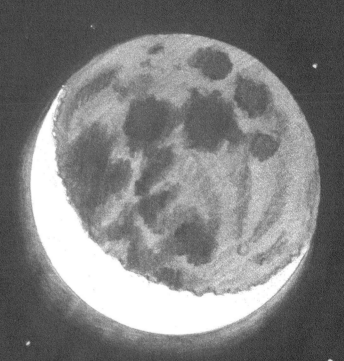

- At the equinox, the Moon climbs into the sky at its steepest angle of the year. That means it quickly rises above the glow of sunset and light pollution, so it can be seen more clearly and earlier than usual. If the Moon is just past new, look for its thin crescent shape right after sunset.

- If the Moon is a waxing crescent, look at the part not lit by the Sun. The equinox is the best time to see the glow of earthshine, when sunlight reflecting off Earth hits the Moon and bounces back. On Earth, we can actually see the Moon's face even though it is in shadow. And with this added earthshine, the sunlit crescent seems larger and brighter, too. People say, "The old Moon is in the new Moon's arms."

SHADOW PLAY

The Maya of Central America were fascinated with the equinoxes. They constructed the Temple of Kukulcán at Chichén Itzá so the late-day Sun on March 21 and September 21 creates a zigzag pattern of light and shadow down one staircase. The pattern looks like a diamondback rattlesnake. Sure enough, at the base of the staircase, a stone-carved snakehead sits in full light at sunset.

The Anasazi people of New Mexico found natural places where the Sun creates special effects on the equinox. In Chaco Canyon, they marked a shaded rock wall that only one sunbeam reaches — and only on the equinoxes in March and September. They drew a spiral on the wall so the sunbeam looks like a dagger approaching a bull's-eye at noon on the equinoxes.

STAR BEAR: A HUNTING ADVENTURE

Long ago, the Micmacs of northeastern North America watched the Big Dipper circle the North Star every year. They used the different positions taken by the circumpolar stars, starting in the spring, to tell the story of a bear hunt. The bear is the bowl of the Big Dipper. Her seven hunters, all birds, are the three handle stars of the Dipper plus four stars in Bootes, the Herdsman. The bear's den is Corona Borealis, the Northern Crown.

In early spring, a keen-eyed chickadee spotted a bear climbing out of her winter's den. The chickadee knew he couldn't take on the bear alone and called his six friends for help — two owls, a blue jay, a passenger pigeon, a gray jay and a robin. The bear caught a glimpse of the hunters and ran for her life. The chase began.

Through all of spring and summer, the hunters tracked the bear across the night sky. In early autumn, the two owls, clumsier fliers than the rest, dropped out of the chase and fell below the horizon. As the nights grew colder, blue jay and pigeon lost the trail and disappeared. Gray jay, chickadee and robin

managed to keep up the chase but grew thin with hunger. In mid-autumn, robin finally cornered the bear. The bear rose up on her hind legs in self-defense, but robin stood his ground and shot her with an arrow. Bear fell on her back and died.

Overcome with hunger, robin jumped onto the bear for a quick bite of fat and was smeared in blood. He flew to a nearby maple tree and tried to shake it off. The blood splattered far and wide, turning the maple leaves red. One patch of blood would not shake off and it stained robin's breast forever.

Finally chickadee caught up with robin. Together, they started a fire, carved up the bear and cooked the meat. When they were ready to eat, gray jay arrived and demanded his full portion. Chickadee and robin were happy to share. While chickadee stirred the pot, gray jay and robin danced around the fire. The hunters were thankful for the food.

The bear's skeleton lies on its back all winter while her spirit moves into another bear asleep in the den. Ever since, when spring returns, a new bear climbs out and the hunt starts all over again.

FOLLOW THAT BEAR!

You can catch each episode of the bear hunt by watching the northern stars once a season in the night sky. You should be able to track the changing positions of the bear — climbing out of its den (spring), running straight across the sky (summer), turning and standing to face its hunters (autumn) and falling down on its back (winter). You should also be able to see when the different hunters quit the chase as their stars fall below the horizon.

Spring 9 p.m.

Summer 9 p.m.

Polaris,
the North Star

Winter 9 p.m.

Autumn 9 p.m.

Looking to the North

☼ SUMMER ☼

Ah, summer. Long days, hot weather and endless afternoons just waiting to be filled with super duper fun. You'll appreciate the sun, and so will your new vegetable garden and composter. The warm sun will also have you outside from morning till night with beach games, field hockey and homemade swings. And if the sun is hiding, there are plenty of indoor activities, too.

VEGETABLE GARDEN

Do you like to have a say in the menu? Why not start a vegetable garden and grow what you like to eat!

You'll need:
a round-mouth shovel
peat moss and/or compost
vegetable seeds
string
sticks for stakes
a hoe or garden rake
a hose and water

1.
Choose a sunny spot, within reach of the hose, for your garden. Stake out the boundaries — 2 m (7 ft.) by 3 m (10 ft.) will be enough for starters. Check your spot with an adult to make sure it's okay to dig there.

2.
Remove the grass with the round-mouth shovel. Use the sod to patch bare spots on the rest of your lawn.

3.
Prepare the soil by turning over the entire area, chopping up and loosening the soil with each shovelful. Dig in peat moss and/or compost to break up and enrich the soil.

4.
Choose vegetable seeds that germinate quickly and have a short growing season. Look on the back of the seed packets for the information on each variety. Peas, lettuce, beans, spinach and Swiss chard are all good. Buy chives and marigold seeds for pest control. Avoid carrots, beets, pumpkin and zucchini. They all require a long growing season. (If you plant in May or early June, you can start these varieties then.)

5.
Using the string and two stakes, mark out each garden row. Using a hoe or the corner of a rake, dig a trough for each variety of seeds. Leave at least 30 cm (12 in.) between rows. You'll need the space for walking and weeding, and the plants need space to grow.

6.
Read the directions on each pack of seeds. The depth for planting varies from vegetable to vegetable. Cover the seeds with soil and tap lightly. Plant the chives and marigold seeds around the edges of the garden. Insects and small animals don't like the smell of these plants and are less likely to help themselves to the lettuce.

7.
Water the entire garden well after planting. Soak the soil with a gentle sprinkle, otherwise you will dislodge the seeds.

8.
Water your garden regularly and generously. The summer heat can dry out and kill the seedlings and plants. It's best to water in the early morning or in the evening when the sun is low in the sky and less water will evaporate.

9.
To help keep pests away, try using some of the wildlife-friendly deterrents on the following page.

MAKE A **SCARECROW**

If you have a garden, you'll likely share some of your garden food with rabbits and raccoons, but a scarecrow and several pinwheels should help you keep most of your crop.

You'll need:

a hammer and nails

a 2 m (7 ft.) long piece of two-by-four wood

a board for the arms

a plastic bag

newspaper

string

a permanent marker

a large old shirt

wild grasses, a sun hat or other things to decorate your scarecrow

1.
Nail the two pieces of wood into a "T" shape.

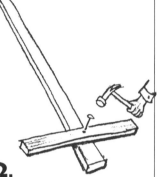

2.
Hammer the "T" into the soil of the garden.

3.
Fill the plastic bag with scrunched-up newspaper. Gather it at the neck and tie it together with a piece of string.

4.
Draw a fierce face on the plastic bag head.

5.
Fasten the head to the top of the "T" with string around the neck.

6.
Using the crossbar of the "T" as arms, dress the scarecrow with a shirt. The flapping shirttails will frighten away some animals.

7.
Jazz up the scarecrow with a sun hat, a fly swatter or a hoe attached to the sleeve and use wild grasses for hair.

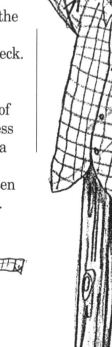

PEST-CONTROL PINWHEELS

You'll need:

a thin piece of plastic
15 cm x 15 cm (6 in. x
6 in.) (plastic windows
from cartons will do)

a ballpoint pen

a ruler

scissors

a thumbtack with a long
needle

a chopstick or thin,
straight stick

1.
Mark the center of the
plastic square with the
ballpoint pen. Label the
four corners 1, 2, 3 and
4, starting with the top
left corner.

2.
Draw a faint "X"
through the midpoint
of the square, joining 1
and 3 with one line and
2 and 4 with
another.

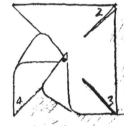

3.
Measure and mark the
point that is halfway
between the midpoint
and each of 1, 2, 3 and
4. Cut along each of
these lines.

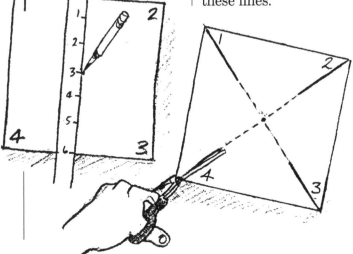

4.
Fold the lower half of
corner 1 to the mid-
point, followed by the
lower half of corner 4,
the upper half of
corner 3 and the upper
half of corner 2.

5.
Push a thumbtack
through all four corner
pieces at the midpoint
of the square and into
the stick.

Make
several
pinwheels
and place them
around the
garden, in the
ground, on
a fence or
attached
to the
scarecrow.

EC WATCH

You can make sure
your garden is
chemical free. If you
get an infestation of
bugs, don't rush off
to buy spray. Many
pests can be chased
away using non-toxic
(non-poisonous)
methods. For
example, try making
a solution of 15 mL
(1 tbsp.) of mild soap
(such as Ivory
Liquid) mixed with
250 mL (1 c.) of
water. Sprinkle it on
bug eggs, larvae or
insects.

SUMMER GARBAGE

If you're at a cottage or camp, far from city recycling programs, you can't forget to reduce, reuse and recycle. Smart shopping and taking recyclables back to the city will help, but you can make your cottage "greener" by making your own composter.

You'll need to build a solid structure that will hold the waste, heat up, let in air, keep out pesky critters and have an opening for stirring and scooping out the compost. Try to make one without buying any materials. Here are some design ideas.

MINI COMPOSTER

Starting small might get your family composting. Use an old, large, rectangular laundry basket. With a nail and hammer, make drainage holes in the bottom. For a lid, use a piece of plywood bigger than the basket. Put a large, heavy rock on top to keep out raccoons. Place in a sunny spot away from the cottage or picnic area.

IT'S A PIT

Select a site for your composting pit. Check with an adult before you start digging — you don't want to unearth cables or the septic tank. Dig a hole about 1 m (3 ft.) square and as deep as possible — up to 1 m (3 ft.). An old screen window makes a good lid. It lets in moisture, lets out smells and keeps out compost thieves.

THE CARPENTER'S COMPOSTER

If you are good with a hammer and nails and have an adult who can help you, try making this wooden composter. Using two-by-fours, make a frame that is 1 m (3 ft.) square and 1 m (3 ft.) tall. The sides can be covered with lattice, plywood with holes drilled in it or chicken wire. A heavy square of plywood makes a good lid. Don't forget the rock "lock."

COMPOST CUISINE

Perfect compost is like a layered salad. You need ingredients from your beach, your lawn, your kitchen and your garden. Start with a layer of stones on the bottom of your composter or in your pit. Next comes a layer of grass cuttings, leaves or trimmings from a hedge or bush. Then a kitchen waste layer. You can compost all vegetable matter, coffee grounds, tea bags, eggshells and unbleached paper. (Don't put in meat, dressings, cereal or dairy products — they smell and attract flies and larger creatures.) Top this with a shovelful of soil. Sprinkle with water. Stir occasionally. Continue to feed your composter all summer long.

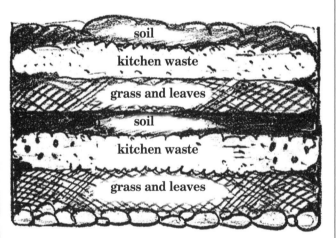

Your compost will have to "cook" for about a year. It's like a good stew — it needs to simmer and mix its flavours for a long time. But don't worry, your garden will be hungry for compost goodness next spring. Shovel the compost, which looks like rich, black soil, onto the flower or vegetable garden. Dig it in before planting time. Compost can also be used to enrich hanging baskets or planters.

SUMMER BIRD FEEDERS

Hanging bird feeders around your house is a great way to see birds up close. Here are three summer bird feeders that are easy to make. See how many different kinds of birds you can attract to your feeders.

SEED FEEDER

You'll need:
a clean cardboard milk or juice carton
scissors
string
birdseed

1.
Punch a hole in the center of the front of your milk carton with scissors and cut out the two sides and the top of a square.

2.
Bend the cut piece out at the bottom and snip it off, leaving a short flap for a perch. Repeat for the opposite side of the carton.

3.
Make a hole through the top of the milk carton with the scissors and thread string through it.

4.
Fill the carton with birdseed and hang your feeder from a tree limb where you can keep an eye on it. Make sure it's well off the ground, but where you can still reach it for refilling. Look for seed-eaters such as rose-breasted grosbeaks and purple finches at your summer seed feeder.

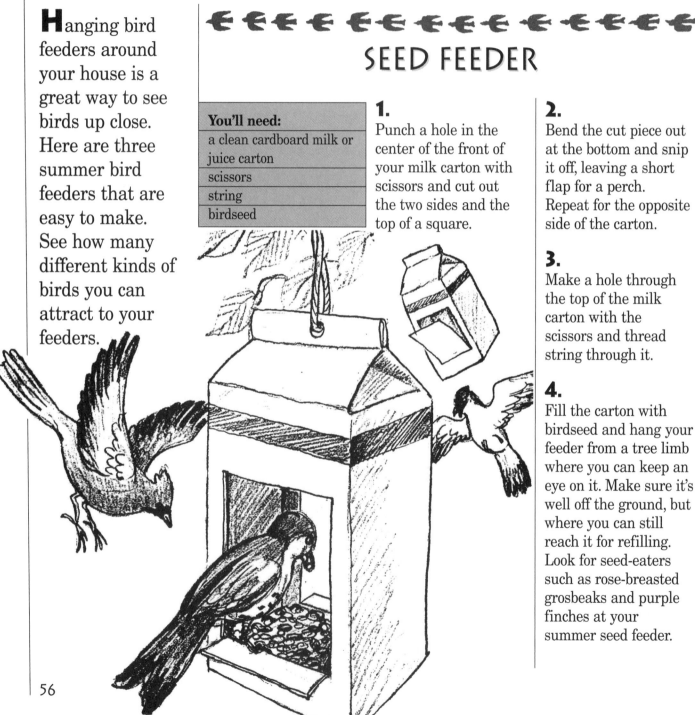

FRUIT FEEDER

You'll need:
a hammer
a strong nail
a piece of partly eaten or spoiled fruit (peach, apple, plum)

1.
Hammer the nail into the side of a tree, above eye level, in a sunny spot you can easily see. Hammer it partway in so the nail is stuck, but it still stands out from the tree.

2.
Punch a piece of fruit onto the nail so it won't fall off.

3.
In the summer's heat, the fruit will start to rot and collect fruit flies. Some birds will come to eat the flies buzzing around the fruit. Others will pick at the fruit itself. When you find another piece of spoiled fruit, jab it onto the nail, too. Look for northern orioles and warblers at your fruit (and fly) feeder.

BIRD FEEDERS AT NIGHT

Don't forget to check all your feeders at night. You may find flying squirrels, luna moths, raccoons, whip-poor-wills and other night-loving creatures helping themselves.

NECTAR FEEDER

You'll need:
red ribbon
a clear, long, thin bottle without a lid (an empty medicine bottle works well)
50 mL (¼ c.) sugar
250 mL (1 c.) hot water
garbage bag tie

1.
Tie the red ribbon around the neck of your bottle. (Hummingbirds are attracted to the color red.)

2.
Add 50 mL (¼ c.) of sugar to 250 mL (1 c.) hot tap water. Stir to dissolve and let the mixture cool.

3.
Pour the sugar and water nectar into the bottle. (Leftover nectar can be kept covered in the fridge for refills.)

4.
With the garbage bag tie, wire the bottle to the top of a strong plant or shrub in a sunny spot you can easily see. If you have a patch of red, orange or pink flowers, wire your feeder near them. Look for ruby-throated hummingbirds hovering at your nectar feeder if you live in the east and rufous hummingbirds if you live in the west.

CALL OF THE WILD

Hunters have always known they can attract wildlife by mimicking their sounds. Northern Native people knew how to call down migrating geese by repeating their honks. Or they could attract moose in dense bush by scraping an antler on spruce bark.

Birds and animals also come to check out squeaky distress calls. They may be friendly and want to help, they may be just curious or they may be predators looking for an easy lunch. On a quiet day, make your own wildlife caller and see who comes to investigate you.

You'll need:
2 Popsicle sticks
a long, wide blade of wild grass (some people use a length of broken cassette tape)
an elastic band

1.
Make sure the Popsicle sticks are clean and dry.

2.
Sandwich a blade of dry grass between the two sticks. Secure one end by wrapping the elastic band around and around it.

3.
Hold the caller up to your mouth, pinch the open end and blow as if playing a harmonica.

4.
To attract wildlife, sit quietly and blow into your caller repeatedly, at the same rhythm and pitch as a crying baby. Waaa Waaa Waaa. See if you attract friend or foe. Blue jays and chickadees may come first. Keep it up and you may spot a fox or hawk.

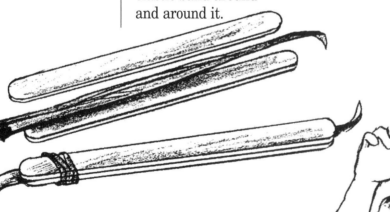

CRY LIKE A LOON

You can make the mournful cry of a loon with only your hands and mouth.

1.

Hold your hands together loosely as if you were just starting to clap. Keep that position, leaving an air pocket between your palms, but tightening your fingers so the air pocket is surrounded.

2.

Press your two thumbs together so your thumbnails face you. Bend the thumb joints down against your cupped hands. You should see a space below your thumb joints and above the base of your thumbs.

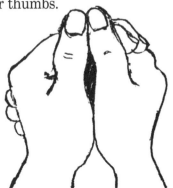

3.

Put the thumb joints to your lips, leaving the hole below the joints free to the air.

4.

Hold your lips loosely, as if you were just getting ready to whistle. Hold back your tongue a little. Blow onto the thumb joints slowly. Adjust the position of your lips until the sound you are producing is full and mournful.

5.

If you hear a loon, return with your own loon call. You may find the loon "talks" back and you can have a conversation. The loon may come closer to see what's up. Then you'll get a good look and see what movements the loon makes to create its call.

SPUD

When the picnic is over and it's time to get moving, SPUD is the game of choice. All you need is a flat playing area, four or more players and a soft ball such as a tennis ball.

PLAYING THE GAME

Ask an adult to whisper a number in the ear of each player. With four players, use numbers 1 to 6; five players, numbers 1 to 7 and so on.

1.
Choose someone to be It.

2.
Gather within touching distance of It. She shouts out a number and throws the ball high in the air. If your number is called, you become It and chase the ball. Everyone else runs as far away as possible.

60

3.

When you've retrieved the ball, yell "SPUD!" All other players freeze. Take three giant steps toward the nearest player and try to hit this person with the ball. Frozen players are allowed to sway and duck to avoid being hit by the ball, but they are not allowed to move their feet.

4.

If you hit a player, that person has one penalty against him, or an S, and he becomes It. If you miss him, *you* get an S. You retrieve the ball, and throw it up and call another number as in step 2.

5.

You are out of the game once you have four penalties or SPUD.

6.

If you call a ghost number — a number not assigned to anyone or a number of a player who is out of the game — you have to chase the ball yourself.

HOOP AND ARROW

Can you hit a moving target? Long ago, this skill could mean the difference between having dinner or going hungry. Native North Americans invented a game to practice their throwing skills when they were relaxed and well fed. You can make this game and see how good your chances of survival would have been before the days of grocery stores.

You'll need:

a circular, plastic lid at least 15 cm (6 in.) across

scissors

a large, empty net bag, like the kind onions come in

twist ties

a thin, branched twig

a knife

modeling clay

feathers for decoration

1.
Use scissors to cut the center out of the plastic lid so that all you have left is a 1.5 cm (⅝ in.) plastic rim. This is the frame of your hoop.

2.
Slip the net bag over your hoop and cut the open end of the bag with scissors so that the netting barely extends beyond the hoop.

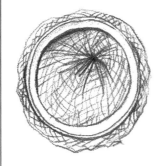

3.
Stretch and tighten the net bag all around the hoop and secure the bag to the hoop with twist ties. You'll have to fold and roll the edges of the open end of the net bag toward the hoop until the fold lies along the rim and then tie it down.

4.
Flatten the twist ties against the plastic rim. Your hoop should now be covered tidily with netting so that the hoop can roll smoothly on its side.

5.
With an adult's help, trim the twig down to a few branches. Cut the tip straight across cleanly with the knife. Avoid a sharp point as this can be dangerous.

6.
Roll a small ball of modeling clay and stick it on the cut end of the twig. The modeling clay ball should be much smaller than the holes in the net bag.

7.
Attach feathers to the ends of the branches on the twig with twist ties.

PLAYING THE GAME

One player rolls the hoop across the ground and
the other tries to throw the arrow into it. The
players take turns seeing who can put the arrow
closest to the center of the net. As you improve
your skills, stand farther
and farther back and
see how you do.

SWING INTO SUMMER

No summer is complete without a swing or two. On hot days, they create wind to blow through your hair. When you're mad or sad, you can shout or sing as you swing.

STEEL-BELTED FUN

BOARD SWING

You'll need:

You'll need:
a piece of board 30 cm x 50 cm (12 in. x 20 in.)
a handsaw
a drill
medium sandpaper
rope
a ladder

You'll need:

You'll need:
a tire or inner tube
3 m (10 ft.) of strong rope
a ladder
a sturdy tree limb

1.

Look around in the shed for an old tire, or take a trip to the dump. Choose a tire that isn't ripped, studded or chained. If you want a soft swing, ask the mechanic at the local garage for an old inner tube. You can have it inflated at the garage or use it floppy.

2.

Ask an adult to help you site your swing. The tree has to be located away from buildings, hydro wires and roads.

3.

Tie a loop knot around the tire (see page 65). Using a ladder, and with help from an adult, tie the rope to a strong right-angled branch using a double half hitch (see page 65). Climb back down again.

4.

Tie the tire so that it swings about a meter (3 ft.) off the ground. Get swinging!

1.

Ask an adult to help you cut the board to the required measurements using a handsaw.

2.

Choose a drill bit a little bigger around than your rope. Ask your adult helper to drill a hole in the middle of each end of the board about 10 cm (4 in.) in from the end.

3.

Using medium sandpaper, hand sand the board so you won't get any slivers. Make sure you sand well along the edges.

4.

Thread the rope through the top of one hole, run the rope along the bottom of the swing and thread the rope through the bottom of the other hole. Pull the rope through until you have equal lengths of rope at each end.

5.

Site your swing, as in the tire swing, allowing about 50 to 75 cm (20 to 30 in.) clearance for your legs. Tie both ropes on the tree branch, using double half hitches. Now, get in the swing!

THE HALF HITCH

The half hitch is the most secure knot for tying a boat to a dock or an anchor rope to a boat or a cleat. Make a double half hitch and your boat will be really safe.

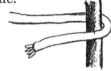

1.

Wrap the rope around a post on the dock or through a cleat.

2.

Pass the working end of the rope under the rope and loop it back over the rope attached to the boat.

3.

Pass the working end under the boat line again and loop back towards the post or cleat. Pull tight.

THE LOOP KNOT

The loop knot is a variation of a slip knot. When used in making a swing, it secures the tire, leaving two pieces of rope free to attach the tire to a tree.

1.

Fold the rope in half. Pass the loop end through the tire.

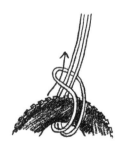

2.

Pass the two loose ends of rope through the loop and pull tight around the tire.

BEACH GAMES

BEACH PADDLEBALL

Take off your shoes and socks and pull on your favorite hat. Here are some games to play on a trip to the beach. Whenever you get too hot, take time out to jump in the water or have a cold drink.

This game of beach table tennis is played by two people. Each player has a table tennis paddle or a beach paddleball paddle, which is larger. Use a ball that is about the size of a table tennis ball but is very bouncy. It is best to play on hard, damp sand near the water's edge.

Drop the ball and serve it as it falls or when it bounces back up. Aim to hit the sand in front of the other player so the ball can be hit back after one bounce. A sidearm swing may be easiest, but underhand and spike shots are also fair. Have a friendly rally and see how long you can keep the ball going back and forth. Then, try to beat your record. It takes a lot of practice to hit the ball well.

PLAYING THE GAME

You can draw a table-tennis-style court in the sand with your heel and play a competitive game. Start with a court about 8 m (25 ft.) long, divided into two 4 m (12½ ft.) ends. The court is for the ball to be shot into — it will bounce well out of the lined area. Players can run outside the lines on their side of the court to return the ball.

1.

The first player serves the ball so it hits the sand in her opponent's half of the court.

2.

The receiving player tries to hit the ball back so it lands on its first bounce in the server's end.

3.

When the server wins a rally, she earns a point.

4.

When the server loses a rally, the serve moves to her opponent, who has a chance to serve and gain points.

5.

Decide before the game whether you will play up to 11 or 15 points.

MORE

67

CROCODILE

Did you ever imagine there was a crocodile under your bed, waiting to take a bite out of you when you stepped on the floor? In this game, you pretend that hungry crocodile is lurking in the sand, ready to bite if the beach ball touches the sand.

Lots of people can play. Throw a beach ball in the air and try to keep it moving for as long as possible without hitting the sand. A player cannot hit the ball twice in a row.

The whole group earns one point for every successful hit.

If the ball does hit the beach, the player who last hit the ball is out — eaten by a croc. Try to set a beach record for the number of points earned before the ball hit the sand.

SNAPPING TURTLES, ALLIGATORS AND CROCODILES

Beaches in some parts of the world are closed to people because of the danger of crocodiles or alligators. If you see a 'gator or a croc, find another swimming hole. Even if you come upon a snapping turtle, stand well back. It will probably leave you alone, but it may bite if it feels hungry or threatened.

DRIBBLE CASTLES

Sit at the edge of the water where the sand is wet — just beyond the reach of the waves. Take a large handful or pailful of dripping sand. Let it slowly dribble into a pile. Create your own lumpy, swirly structure, moving in a circular motion. It won't look like a conventional castle, but it will look great when it dries. Don't forget to keep the sand really wet while you're working with it.

SCULPTURES

Sand sculptures are easy to make using your hands and a shovel. Mound moist sand into the desired shape, packing the sand firmly with your hands. Your own creative genius will tell you what you can sculpt in the sand, but here are a few suggestions to get you started.

SAND DINOSAURS

Recreate the Mesozoic era (the age of the dinosaurs) complete with prehistoric creatures. *Stegosaurus* looks awesome in the sand; so does *Tyrannosaurus rex*, or the long, smooth tail of *Apatosaurus*. Use twigs and driftwood to complete the landscape.

SAND MONSTERS

Frighten away the tourists with Everglades creatures. Snakes, alligators, crabs and a crouching panther will make a swampy scene. Add a tangle of sticks and twigs with some greenery to create a mangrove habitat.

SCHOOLS OF BEACH FISH

Go fishing without the rod and reel. Fish appear to swim through the sand, with pebble scales that catch the sun. Make an entire school.

FEEDING THE GULLS

You can befriend the local gull flock with your stale bread and leftover toast. Collect a plate of scrap bread after each meal. At the end of each day, go down to the water's edge and call, "Here gully, gully, gully." Wait for the first gull to fly by and toss it a small morsel. Within seconds, you'll have every gull around sweeping over your head. Try to throw the bread high enough so the gulls will catch it in the air.

Begin every feeding session with the call, "Here gully, gully, gully." You'll be surprised how quickly the gulls learn to recognize your voice and associate it with dinnertime!

PEBBLES IN THE SAND

Wari is an Egyptian board game that's more than a thousand years old. The game spread to Africa and then traveled with African slaves to America and the West Indies. Wari boards have been dug in the soil or made from wood, stone or pottery. To have your own instant wari board, all you need are 48 small pebbles for counters, a sandy beach and a friend.

GETTING READY

Choose a flat section of beach where the sand is moist, not wet. Scoop out 12 holes about the same depth and distance apart as the holes in an egg carton. This forms the wari board. Place four stones in each hole.

PLAYING THE GAME

1.

Sit on opposite sides of the wari board. The six holes directly in front of each player is her home base. The aim of the game is to capture the counters in your opponent's holes.

70

2.

Player one picks up four counters from any hole in her row and places or "sows" one in each of her next four holes to the right (or counterclockwise).

3.

Player two takes a turn as above. Continue taking turns until the last counter sown must go into one of the opponent's holes. If the hole already contains two or three counters, the player captures the counters in that hole, scoops all the counters out and sets them aside. If the hole to the left or right of this hole contains two or three counters, she captures them also.

4.

If there are 12 or more counters in a hole that a player ends in, the player picks up the counters and sows them all the way around the board. Starting with the next hole to the right, she sows one counter per hole, skipping the hole they were removed from.

5.

If the hole contains any number of counters other than two, three or twelve, the new counter is simply added into the hole.

6.

If your opponent's row is empty, you must, on your next turn, try to sow at least one counter on her side. If this can't be done, or if a player has no counters left, the game is over and the last person to move gets all the remaining counters on the board. Count them up and the person with the most is the winner.

TIP

As you sow your counters, try to make it impossible for your opponent to land in one of your holes with two or three counters.

PERMANENT WARI

If you want a permanent wari game, use an egg carton as a board. Pebbles, dried beans or shells make good counters. Store your 48 counters inside the egg carton between games.

TREASURE HUNT

A treasure hunt is a good event to organize if you're having friends of different ages over. All you need is a shovel, a pencil and paper, and treasure. The treasure should include energy food and drinks because everyone will be hungry by the time it's unearthed!

The best treasure hunts get friends working together, not against one another. If you can, wrap the loot well and bury it in the ground. The organizer of a hunt can't play but can dig into the spoils at the end.

GETTING READY

1.

Choose a big playing area and decide where to start the hunt and where to bury the loot. A good burying place is a dug-up garden, in a spot where there are no plants growing.

2.

Survey the whole playing area and choose 10 places to hide clues. In each place, you will leave a clue that should lead the treasure hunters to the next clue.

3.

Write 10 clues. Your clues should be hard but solvable by your hunters. If you want players to look under the seat of the swing, for instance, write a word scramble for "swing seat," draw a map or write a riddle such as "where one seat meets another" — it all depends on the age of your treasure hunters.

4.

When no one is watching, lay out all your clues in order, except the first one. Then walk through the sequence to make sure every clue is in the right place. Bury the treasure and invite your friends over.

5.

Give them the first clue and a shovel. Be sure you're around at the end to share the treasure!

SKULL AND CROSSBONES

No treasure hunt is complete without a pirate theme. While you're planning the hunt, others can be making a traditional skull-and-crossbones flag, eye patches or bandannas so they can really act the part.

BOOTIN'

If you're a hockey fanatic who lives and breathes the game all year long, bootin' is the game for you. The equipment is simple: hockey sticks, a soft ball the size of a melon and boots, of course. Boots act as shin pads and feet protectors.

PLAYING THE GAME

Set out the boundaries of the play area, whether it is a lawn, beach, park or school-yard. A rectangular space is ideal but not necessary. Trees, rocks, buildings and hazards should be declared out of bounds.

Set up a goal the size of a regular hockey net at either end of the play area.

1.
Divide into two teams of three to eight players each. Use different kinds of clothing to tell the teams apart — one team plays in T-shirts, the other in swimsuits.

2.
Teams choose a goalie and one or two players to play defense. The rest are forwards.

3.
The ball is placed on the ground in the center of the play area. Two players, one from each team, "face off" saying together, "one, two, three, go" and try to gain possession of the ball.

4.
Players try to get the ball past the goalie of the opposite team. Each goal counts for one point.

RULES

- High-sticking is not allowed. The blade of the stick must stay below the knees and the handle of the stick below the shoulders.

- If a player is hit with a stick anywhere except on the boots, he can take a free shot on the goalie, 10 paces out from the net. All the other players stand aside.

- For safety, players are not allowed to raise the ball off the ground higher than their knees.

HOCKEY HYDRATION

Even on ice, hockey players get hot and thirsty. Don't forget to drink plenty of water when playing bootin' or any other outdoor game.

5.

When one team hits the ball out of bounds, a member of the other team places the ball on the boundary line where it went out and shoots it back into play.

6.

In bootin' there are no periods or intermissions. The game continues until everyone is exhausted. Each game ends in a tie, no matter how many goals have been scored. When ready to stop, one player calls, "last goal ties."

PICTURE IT

How are your drawing skills? Whether you are a clever artist or not doesn't really matter. You'll need only a pencil, big pieces and small slips of paper, and a good imagination to play this word-drawing game.

PLAYING THE GAME

Divide into two teams. Each team thinks up some expressions, such as "marshmallow roast," and writes each of these on a slip of paper. There should be one expression for every member of the opposite team. If the teams are made up of different age groups, choose easier expressions for the younger kids.

One player at a time is given a slip of paper by the opposing team. When it's your turn, read what's on the paper to yourself, then put it away. On a big piece of paper, draw pictures to make your team say the expression out loud. You are not allowed to print letters or numbers or act anything out. Your teammates can ask questions, but you can only answer by drawing pictures. You have three minutes to get your team to identify the expression. Then a player on the opposite team tries to illustrate a different expression.

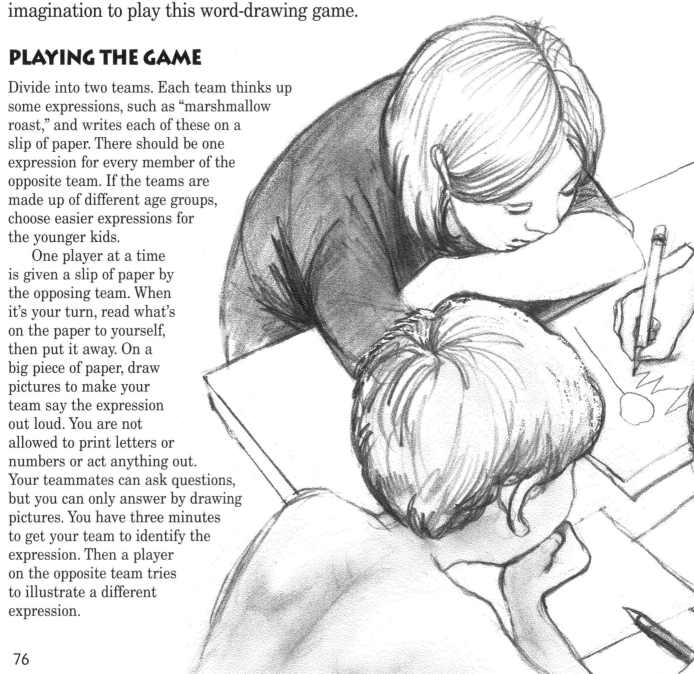

TIPS

- When another team member is drawing, you need to concentrate. Make lots of good guesses about what the drawings might mean.

- If a team member who is drawing seems stuck, ask helpful questions such as, "What kind of expression is it?" Then your teammate can draw a TV screen to mean a TV show title, a person singing to indicate a song title, and so on.

- Work out team symbols for "yes," "no" and "you're getting warm." You may also need a drawing symbol for numbers.

- When you are writing down expressions for the other team, remember that including a lot of nouns, or naming words, makes a definition easier. Verbs and adverbs, which describe actions, make them harder.

SOME SUMMERY EXPRESSIONS

- Last one in is a dirty rotten egg!
- Everyone out of the pool!
- It's hot outside
- Skinny dip
- "Fire's Burning"
- "If You're Happy and You Know It, Clap Your Hands"

MIDWAY GAMES

Practice up for your next trip to a fair playing these games of accuracy.

MUFFIN-PAN MIDWAY

Bring the excitement of the midway to your home.

You'll need:
an old 12-hole muffin pan
a permanent marker
some string
4 pennies
a pen and some paper

1.
Turn the muffin pan on its side so there are four holes across and three down.

2.
Use the marker to label each hole with a number value as shown.

3.
Lean the muffin pan against a wall on a carpeted floor or on top of a towel.

4.
Mark a starting line on the floor with a piece of string 2 m (6 ft.) long. Move the string farther away from the muffin pan if the game is too easy.

PLAYING THE GAME

Players take turns kneeling behind the starting line and trying to throw pennies into the pan. Gentle underhand throws usually work best. Keep score after each turn. The first person to score 1000 wins.

TIDDLYWINKS

Be the first one to shoot all your winks into a cup and you've won the game. Sounds easy, but the winks don't always cooperate. Practice will improve your accuracy.

You'll need:
assorted buttons and coins
small margarine tub
flannel sheet
some string

GETTING READY

- Each player needs four winks and a shooter. For winks, use different colored buttons, about 2 cm (³/₄ in.) across, for each player. Use a larger button or a coin about 3 cm (1 in.) across as a shooter.

- Use a small margarine tub, measuring 3 cm (1 in.) tall, for the target cup.

- A flannel sheet, laid flat on a hard floor, makes the best tiddlywinks play area.

- Place the target cup in the middle of the sheet. Use a piece of string to mark a curved starting line, 0.5 m (1½ ft.) away from the cup.

PLAYING THE GAME

1.
Players line up their winks on the starting line.

2.
To start the game, each player takes one shot toward the cup, leaving his wink where it lands.

3.
The player whose wink is closest to the cup goes first. He takes another shot with the same wink. If his wink lands in the cup, he starts again with a second wink. If he misses the cup, his turn is over.

4.
Play continues, clockwise, until one person has all four winks in the cup. Sort out the winks and play again.

5.
When the game is over, store the winks in the margarine tub.

SHOOTING WINKS

Hold the shooter between the thumb and index finger and press the shooter down on the edge of the wink. The wink will flick away.

JACKS

Gather a group of friends together for a game of jacks. All you need is a set of five jacks, a small bouncy ball and a flat, hard surface. Learn each trick, progressing from easy to difficult. Once you've mastered the basics, challenge your friends with your own variations.

PLAYING THE GAME

Before beginning, players agree on which tricks they will attempt and in what order. Decide who goes first by taking turns throwing all five jacks up in the air and catching as many as possible on the back of your hand. Then toss the caught jacks up again and try to catch them in the cup of your palm. Whoever ends up with the most jacks goes first. She plays until she fails to complete a trick properly. The first person to complete all the tricks is the winner.

ONES

Throw the jacks on the ground. Using one hand, toss the ball into the air, pick up one jack and catch the ball after the first bounce. Transfer the jack to the other hand and repeat until all five are picked up. You are out if you drop a jack or touch one that you are not attempting to pick up.

TWOS, THREES, FOURS AND FIVES

Played as in Ones, jacks are picked up two, three, four and finally five at a time. In each trick, the jacks are picked up in batches. For example, in Twos, two groups of two jacks are picked up, followed by the remaining one; in Threes, three jacks are picked up together and then the remaining two.

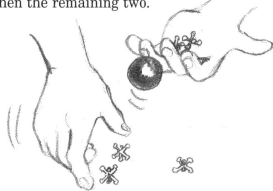

CRACK THE EGG

Throw the jacks on the ground. Toss the ball in the air, pick up one jack, tap it on the ground, "cracking the egg," and catch the ball after the first bounce. Continue until all five have been picked up. Now play as in Twos, tapping the jack twice, then play as in Threes, tapping three times and so on. Did you drop any jacks? If so, you're out.

HOMEMADE JACKS

If you have a small bouncy ball but no jacks, you can substitute five small objects, such as pebbles or acorns.

WHEN JACKS WERE BONES

The game's the same, but the name's changed. Ancient Greeks threw the knucklebones of sheep on the ground, "read" them and predicted future events. In the thirteenth century, during the Trojan War, the Greek leader Palamedes and his soldiers played a game using knucklebones. Bone games have been popular for centuries in Asia, Polynesia, Russia and across the Arctic. Kids in Pompeii played them almost 2000 years ago!

81

MAKE A NIGHT SKY DOME

In the Middle Ages, Europeans used to paint night sky scenes on the domed ceilings of their buildings. You can make a night sky dome to hang in a window or from your ceiling and see your favorite constellations indoors, day or night.

★ ★

You'll need:
a large plastic bowl
petroleum jelly, such as Vaseline
125 mL (½ c.) flour
15 mL (1 tbsp.) salt
250 mL (1 c.) water
newspaper, torn into strips 1 cm (½ in.) wide
scissors
poster or tempera paints, including black
a paintbrush
white glue (optional)
thread

1.
Turn the bowl upside down and thinly coat the outside with petroleum jelly.

2.
In another container, mix flour, salt and water to make a smooth, runny paste. (Covered with plastic wrap, this paste will last in the fridge for a few days.)

3.
Dip the newspaper strips into the paste one at a time, using your fingers to spread the paste evenly. Place the strips on the bowl to cover it, overlapping the strips and smoothing the paste as you go.

4.
Repeat step 3 to make four layers, placing the strips in a different direction for each layer.

5.

Near the lip of the bowl, poke a small hole in your dome. Let your work sit for several days, until completely dry.

6.

When dry, the dome should easily lift off the bowl. Once separated, wipe any petroleum jelly off the dome with a damp, soapy cloth. If the dome's lip is rough, trim it with scissors, rub paste along the lip and lay a newspaper strip along the paste. Smooth your repair with paste and let it dry.

7.

Paint the outside of the dome any color you like and let it dry.

8.

Paint the inside of the dome black and let it dry.

9.

Paint white or yellow stars inside the dome for your favorite constellations. When dry, brush with a thin layer of glue for a glossy finish, if you like.

10.

Tie thread through the hole you made in step 5. Hang your night sky dome from the ceiling.

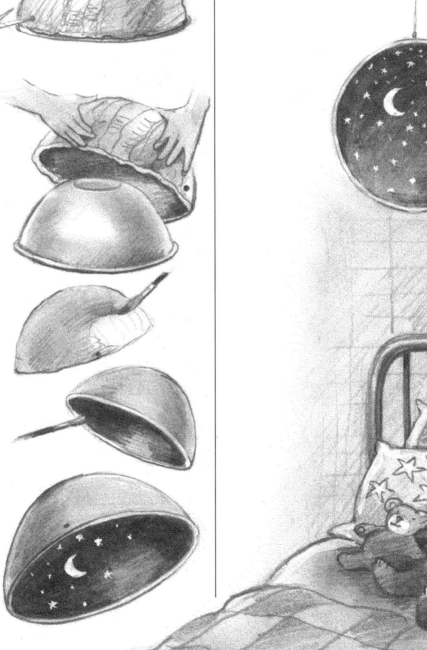

WHAT TO LOOK FOR IN THE SUMMER SKY

Your hosts of the summer sky are three bright stars — Vega, Altair and Deneb. Together they make up the Summer Triangle. Look for the triangle in the east on a June evening, moving to overhead as the season progresses.

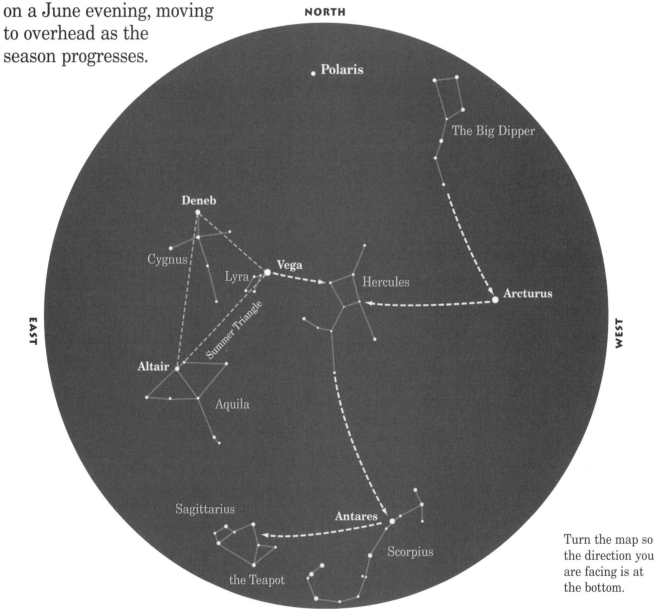

Turn the map so the direction you are facing is at the bottom.

VEGA

The brightest star in the Summer Triangle, Vega is bluish white. It is in the constellation Lyra, the Harp.

ALTAIR

The second-brightest star in the triangle, Altair is white. Altair is in the constellation Aquila, the Eagle.

DENEB

The dimmest star of the Summer Triangle, Deneb would be the brightest if it were not so far away. It is actually 60 000 times brighter than our Sun. Deneb is the tail of the large constellation Cygnus, the Swan. The head of Cygnus lies between Altair and Vega. Some people call Cygnus "the Northern Cross."

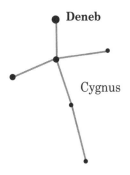

Once you have found the Summer Triangle, you can star hop to find …

THE KEYSTONE

Between Vega and Arcturus, look for four stars in a wedge or keystone shape. This is the body of Hercules, the Strongman. His feet are to the north and his arms to the south, making his figure kneel upside down in the sky.

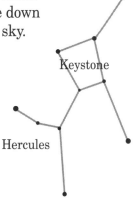

ANTARES

Look directly south of Hercules, almost to the horizon, to find the supergiant orange-red star Antares, the heart of Scorpius. Farther south and east of Antares, look for the creature's nasty hooked stinger.

THE TEAPOT

To the east of Scorpius but still well to the south, look for the outline of a teapot in the sky. The stars that make the teapot also make the eye, bow and arrow of Sagittarius, the Archer.

Sagittarius

THE SUMMER SOLSTICE

Every day from late December to June, the Sun rises and sets a little farther north along the horizon. But about June 21, the Sun seems to stop moving north. It rises in the northeast and sets in the northwest, seemingly in the same spots for several days. After the pause, the Sun travels south to reach another standstill, or solstice, on or about December 21. Earth's elongated orbit around the Sun plus the tilt of Earth's axis produces the standstill effect. At each solstice, Earth is rounding one of the long ends of its orbit. As we swing around the end, neither Earth nor the Sun seems to move. The same standstill effect occurs when you toss a ball in the air. The ball seems to freeze at the top of your throw before it falls back down.

THE MILKY WAY

The Milky Way, our home galaxy, is made up of about 400 billion stars. It spins through the universe like a giant pinwheel with long spiral arms that arch away from a star-packed central bulge. Our sun is more than two-thirds out from the center of the galaxy on one of its arms.

From Earth, the Milky Way looks like a misty band of light in the night sky. In summer, Earth faces the middle of our galaxy, so the Milky Way is brighter than at any other time of year. The center of the galaxy is in the direction of the spout of the Teapot in Sagittarius. If you look there, you'll see patches of dust and gas so thick they block out the starlight shining behind them. Many of these dust clouds, or nebulae, are nurseries where stars are being born.

HUBBLE'S OWN TELESCOPE

Astronomer Edwin Hubble proved that the Milky Way was not the only galaxy in the universe. He photographed the Andromeda Galaxy with a telescope and showed it was made up of billions of stars, just like our Milky Way.

THE HISTORY OF OUR GALAXY (AND THE UNIVERSE, TOO)

The distant past: The whole universe may be smaller than the head of a pin. Who knows? Space and time don't exist — yet!

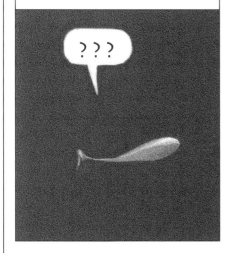

About 13 billion years ago: The universe expands rapidly outwards. Space and time begin.

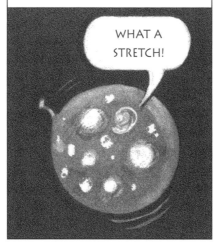

... a few seconds later: The whole universe is a raging fireball, filled with hot, glowing, colliding electrons, protons and photons.

... 300 000 years later: The temperature in space cools and hydrogen atoms form. Space becomes transparent for the first time.

Up to the present: Gas and dust swirl through space, sometimes collecting into large clouds and collapsing to form stars, planets and even galaxies like our Milky Way.

Distant future: Will the universe, time and space grow forever or end in a big crunch?

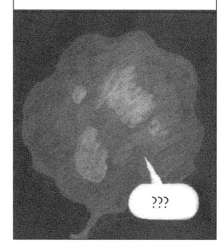

MILKY WAY STORIES

In 1609, Galileo pointed his telescope on the Milky Way and discovered it was made up of millions of stars. Today, scientists think migrating birds use the light from these stars to navigate. The Estonians of northern Europe have an old tale that links migrating birds to the Milky Way.

Lindu, beautiful daughter of the sky god Uko, took care of all birds on their spring and fall flights. Many young men wanted to marry her, but Lindu found none as exciting as her birds.

North Star was the first to propose. He arrived in a fine carriage drawn by six dark horses and laden with ten gifts. But Lindu was not interested because she knew he preferred to stay in one place all the time. Then Moon pulled up in his silver coach with ten horses and twenty gifts. But Lindu turned him down because he traveled along the same well-worn path every night. When Sun appeared in a golden chariot drawn by twenty strong red horses and thirty gifts, Lindu rejected him, too. She knew Sun walked the same old path Moon did, except by day. Lindu found all the young men boring.

Then Northern Lights drove up in a diamond carriage drawn by a thousand white horses and carrying gifts beyond counting. He was brash and brilliant; he came and went as he pleased. Dazzled, Lindu fell in love. Northern Lights told her to prepare for their wedding and that he would return — and then he disappeared into the north.

Lindu put on her bridal dress and waited … through autumn, winter, spring and into next summer. She stared north, growing more and more unhappy, never thinking of her friends the birds. As autumn approached again, Uko felt he must do something to help his daughter and the birds. He called upon the wind to carry Lindu into the sky. There she remains, her long, white veil shimmering as the Milky Way, directing the birds in their journeys. But she stares north, trying to catch a glimpse of Northern Lights. When she sees him, she waves. And occasionally he waves back.

A WELL-LIT ROAD

The idea that the Milky Way's band of light was a "way" or road runs through many old stories.

- The Norse of Scandinavia said the Milky Way was the path that warrior ghosts traveled to reach Valhalla, their afterworld.

- The Yup'ik of eastern Siberia and western Alaska said the Milky Way was the snowshoe track left by Raven after he created people.

- The Armenians said the Milky Way was a trail of straw dropped by a thief.

- Some ancients said the Milky Way was a celestial waterway. The Egyptians called it a heavenly Nile River, the Hindus a Ganges River in the sky and the Hebrews a river of light.

◗ FALL ◖

The summer is over, and the days are getting shorter. The fall air is getting cooler, too. But that doesn't mean the fun is over! It's still warm enough for a game of Frisbee golf or capture the flag. And nature is still putting on a beautiful display — try making a wildlife blind for some furry friends or spying on an anthill. You can even make a worm farm! Once the cooler weather rolls in, be prepared with fun games to play when you're hanging out inside.

WILDLIFE BLIND

Seeing a wild animal up close in its natural habitat can be very exciting. Get a closer, longer look at wild animals by constructing a wildlife blind beside a marsh, on the beach, in a meadow or at the edge of the forest.

You'll need:
cloth 3 m x 1 m (10 ft. x 3 ft.)
scissors
string
camouflage material, such as sticks and leaves

1.
Select cloth that will blend in with the surroundings, such as an old piece of burlap, a brown bedspread or an old green tablecloth.

2.
Choose a site for the blind where you have observed animals or birds. Bulrushes, shrubs, tall grasses or sand dunes are great natural hiding places.

3.
Make holes in the four corners of the cloth with the scissors.

4.
Cut four pieces of string about 50 cm (20 in.) long. Pull a piece of string through each corner opening and knot one end of the string.

5.
Cut four or five 25 cm (10 in.) slits in the cloth. These will be your peepholes.

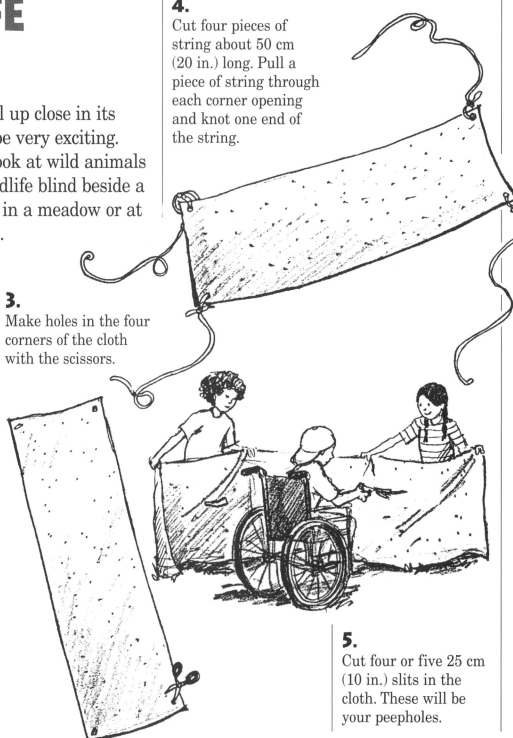

6.
Wrap the cloth around one side of the bulrushes, shrubs or tall grasses close to the ground. Use the strings to secure it in place.

9.
After several days, your blind will become part of the scenery, and local wildlife will no longer notice it is there.

10.
Snuggle in behind the blind and quietly wait for any passersby. Use the peepholes to see if there are any wild creatures in the area.

7.
Use grasses, sticks and leaves that you find around your site to camouflage your blind, making it blend in with the surroundings.

8.
If your blind is behind a sand dune, you'll need three sturdy sticks to jab into the sand. Make a V with the sticks, securing the ends of the cloth on the outside two sticks.

GAME TRAILS

If you look closely at the ground in meadows or forests, you can see little paths used by animals. These are called game trails. They can be used by all sizes of creatures, from mice to coyotes, to travel safely from the cover of the forest to the nearest watering hole. Try to find a game trail on your property and make your blind within view of it. What animals travel on your trail? Make sure you stay quiet and still, especially if you see a skunk.

WORM FARM

If you're out on a night prowl, why not look for some worms? Earthworms can be kept for a few weeks in a jar. All you have to do is duplicate the environment in which they were living and provide them with fresh food and water. The key to success is care. In a few short weeks, you can have a fascinating snarl of tunnels to watch and — if you're lucky — baby worms. Before it gets really cold, you can add your worms to a composter and they will help create new soil for next summer's tomatoes.

You'll need:
the largest jar you can find — a 4 L (1 gallon) condiment jar works well
loose soil
sand
water
leaves
lettuce
a flashlight
a clean yogurt or margarine tub
a brown paper bag
scissors
sticky tape

1.
Fill your jar three-quarters full with layers of loose garden or woodland soil and sand. Do not pack it in. Sprinkle lightly with water. Place several leaves on the top and a few bits of lettuce.

2.
Keep your worm farm in a cool place, such as a shed or basement. Choose a spot away from sunlight and too much heat. Now you're ready to hunt for worms.

3.
Worms can be found easily after a rain or at night using a flashlight. They live in cool, damp places so look under logs, at the edge of a woods or dig in the garden. Collect 4 to 6 worms, along with a handful of soil, in the yogurt tub.

4.

Place the worms in their prepared home and leave them undisturbed for a few days to let them settle.

5.

Make a protective paper sleeve to slip over the outside of the jar to keep out light and heat. This is easily done with a brown paper bag, scissors and some tape. Make it loose enough so you can slip it off for viewing the worms.

6.

Replace the lettuce leaves every other day.

7.

Return the worms to their original home or add them to your composter when you're finished watching your wormery.

FOOD AND WATER

Worms will eat a variety of garden leaves so try several kinds and note what they like and what they leave behind. You can also use carrot tops or cabbage. Remove any rotting food from the jar.

Worms need water, too, but don't want to live in a swamp. Worms breathe through their skin and will drown if the soil is too wet. Keep the soil damp by misting the inside of the jar with a spray bottle or letting a few drops drip from your finger.

WORM WATCHING

Now prepare for some serious worm watching. You will be able to see their tiny hairlike "feet," called setae, as the worms slither up the side of the jar. Are they moist and slimy? Which end is which? The mouth opens and shuts as they move along. Do they ever go backward? Tap on the outside of the jar and see what they do. What does the soil look like after a few days? Have the worms mixed it up into a zigzag of sand and soil?

Worms are blind but they are still sensitive to light. They are nocturnal (active at night), slipping back into the soil by dawn. That's a good way for them to avoid the hunting beaks of robins. Use a flashlight to check on your worm farm at night. Do they react to the light?

Worms are also deaf but they can still sense vibration. When they feel the footfalls of birds or animals, they retreat into their burrows.

TELLING TIMES

Long before people had watches or digital clocks, our bodies told us the time of day when our stomachs growled or our eyelids wouldn't stay open. We still don't need a watch to tell us it's mealtime or bedtime — our bodies let us know. It's all the in-between times we need watches for. Make a sundial so you can tell the time without a watch.

You'll need:
a sharp pencil
a piece of string 15 cm (6 in.) long
a piece of wood or thick cardboard about 30 cm (12 in.) long and about 15 cm (6 in.) wide
a squared piece of thin cardboard, such as the side of a cereal box
a ruler
scissors
white glue

1.

Start by making the base of the sundial. Tie the pencil to one end of the string. Hold the free end of the string under your thumb halfway down the edge of the piece of wood. Pull the string tight and draw a semi-circle on the wood from the top to the bottom around your thumb. Now, draw a straight line from where you held your thumb to the opposite edge of the wood.

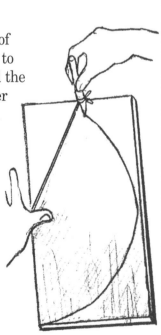

2.

Next, make the "hand" of the sundial, called the gnomon. Pick up the piece of thin cardboard by one corner and mark 15 cm (6 in.) along the bottom and 15 cm (6 in.) up the side. Cut diagonally between your two marks to make a triangle.

3.

On one of the shorter sides, draw a straight line about 1 cm (1/2 in.) up from the edge and fold along that line to make a flap. You should now have a triangular card with a flap on the bottom.

4.

Glue the flap onto your base as shown.

5.

Place your sundial on a flat spot outside where it'll get full sun all day. Line it up so the gnomon points north. (You can do this at night with the North Star. The North Star is easy to find because it's the one that is "pouring" out of the Big Dipper.)

6.

Now, make the dial of your sundial. Using a watch, mark where the shadow from the gnomon falls on the base every hour and label each mark with its time. Do this all day until you've marked all the hours from sunup to sundown. From now on, you'll be able to leave your watch inside on sunny days and read the time from your sundial.

NATURAL WATCHES

Just as you have an inner clock to tell when it's lunchtime or bedtime, so do some plants. Learn to read some of these natural clocks.

Marigold flowers, for instance, open each morning by 7 o'clock. Blue chicory and pickerelweed close up at noon. The white water-lily shuts tight every afternoon at 4 o'clock and the marigold closes by 7 p.m. Look around and you'll be able to find other examples of plant clocks to help you tell the time.

Some plants open up on schedule every day even if it's not sunny. When you find a plant clock, cover it with a pail and peek in to see if it still opens and closes on time, even though it's in the dark.

Look for animal clocks, too. Deerflies may bug you after 9 a.m., horseflies at 2 p.m. and pesky mosquitoes by 8 p.m. You can even teach animals to tell you the time. If you put honey on a spoon in the same place at the same time every day, bees will get to expect it and come buzzing — and they won't be late.

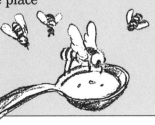

SPYING INTO AN ANTHILL

Have you ever left a picnic lunch on the ground and returned to find your sandwich being carried off by ants? Next time, follow that food back to the anthill. You can construct your own anthill to get an inside look at their busy lives.

You'll need:
a large clear plastic pop bottle
a handsaw
a rectangular-shaped rock, a bit smaller than the bottle
plastic wrap
sticky tape
a tray
a trowel or large spoon
a plastic bag
a pail
a piece of paper
a small piece of wet sponge
a cotton ball
a small piece of fine fabric
an elastic band
an old towel

1.
Ask an adult to help you cut the bottom off your plastic pop bottle with the saw.

2.
Turn the bottle topside-down and put the rock inside the bottle as shown. The rock will fill the center of the bottle and force the ants to construct their nests and tunnels against the walls of the bottle where you can see them working.

3.
Stretch plastic wrap over the bottom opening and tape it there so it forms a complete seal.

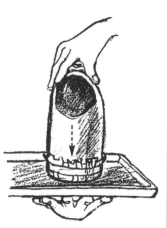

4.
Center the tray face down on the bottom of the bottle. Holding the neck of the bottle with one hand and pushing on the bottom of the tray with the other hand, turn the bottle right-side-up so that it is sitting in the middle of the tray.

5.
Carry the trowel, plastic bag and pail to your local anthill.

6.
Cut deep into the top of the hill with your trowel. Gently catch some of the scurrying ants in your plastic bag. Search for ants carrying cocoons — they look like pieces of dry rice. Look for a queen ant, too — she'll have a much larger body than regular worker ants.

When you've collected about 20 ants, tie the top of the bag shut. Collect some of the earth from the anthill in your pail. You'll need enough to fill more than half your pop bottle.

7.

Return to your pop bottle. Make a funnel with the piece of paper and pour the earth into the bottle so it falls around the rock.

8.

Poke the piece of wet sponge into the bottle neck and down onto the top of the earth.

9.

Drop in some crumbs from your picnic for good measure.

10.

Pour the ants from the collecting bag in next and quickly poke a cotton ball in the neck after them.

11.

Cover the top of the bottle with a piece of fabric held in place with the elastic band.

12.

Drape the towel over the whole bottle and leave it in darkness.

13.

Once a day, take off the towel, open the top and refresh the food supply. Add a few water drops to the sponge. Check to see if the ants have done any construction.

14.

After about three days, you should start to see tunnels and rooms as if you were looking into an anthill. You should see where they take their food and how they tend their young.

15.

After a couple of weeks of spying on your ants, carry your tray back to the original anthill and rip the plastic off the bottom of the bottle. Let the ants return to their relatives — and to their hard work, including picnic-robbing.

ANT FOOD

You know ants like picnics. But what are their preferred foods? Try giving your ants a small bit of cereal, a shredded piece of meat, a few seeds of grass, a few grains of sugar and so on. Which do they gobble up first? You may be surprised!

WINDSOCK FORECASTING

You'll be the best forecaster around if you make this windsock to measure the wind's direction and strength.

You'll need:
a ¾ m (2 ft.) stick or wood dowel, 1 cm (½ in.) thick
a 2 cm (¾ in.) wood screw and screwdriver
needlenosed pliers
75 cm (2½ ft.) wire from a coat hanger
scissors
a 1 m x 1 m (3 ft. x 3 ft.) square of nylon fabric
a needle and thread

1.

Screw the wood screw partway into one end of the stick so the screw head sticks out about 1 cm (½ in.).

2.

With the pliers, twist one end of the wire into a small, loose loop around the stick about 15 cm (6 in.) below the screw.

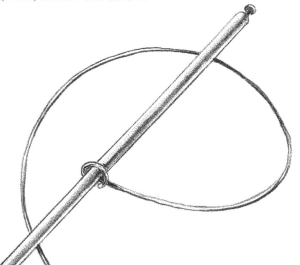

3.

With the pliers, bend the next 30 cm (1 ft.) of wire into an arc from the loop up to the screw neck.

4.

Make a second loop around the screw, loose enough to turn on the neck but tight enough not to slip off the head.

5.

Bend the remaining wire into another arc back down to your starting point to complete a wire circle with the arc you made in step 3. Make a final loop around the stick below your first loop. You should be able to hold the stick and swing the wire frame around it.

6.

Fold the nylon square in half, good side facing in. Center the wire frame on the nylon at one end of the folded fabric. Cut through both pieces of nylon to make identical triangles that are wider than the wire frame at one end and then taper to a point (or tail) at the other.

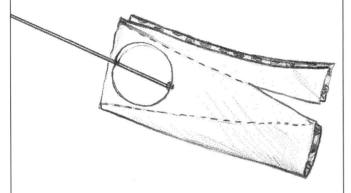

7.

Sew the long sides of the triangles together. Tie off the sewing on each side just before the ends to leave a small hole in the tail of the sock.

8.

Turn the sock right side out. Pull the wide mouth end of the sock into the frame and fold 5 cm (2 in.) of the nylon back over the wire. Fold again to make a hem and stitch the sock onto the frame so it swings easily.

9.

With the help of an adult, mount the windsock by wiring or nailing the stick on the top of a pole or roof. The sock should spin freely.

WILD WEATHER

Will winter bring frosty mornings with piles of snow? Or will it stay mild and green outside? Some people say they can forecast winter weather by observing wildlife in the fall. Check this list of plant and animal lore to decide what kind of winter is in store for you.

If you notice these signs in the fall, winter may be cold, severe and long:

Deer grow extra thick fur and squirrels' tails grow more bushy.

Muskrats build new houses.

The hair of wooly bear caterpillars grows so the black stripes are wider than the brown ones.

Onion skins grow unusually thick.

Rose bushes bend over, heavy with rosehips.

Squirrels and chipmunks are extra busy storing their piles of nuts and seeds.

The tops of spruce and pine trees have a lot of cones.

Beavers build their winter lodges unusually early.

FALL TRAVELERS

Did you know that monarch butterflies migrate south for the winter, just like birds do? In the autumn, they fly to southern California and Mexico. There they hang on trees by the millions and doze the winter through. In spring, the females travel to the southern states where they lay their eggs. Those eggs hatch and the adults go farther north to lay eggs again. By the time you see a monarch in the summer, it may be the great-great-grandchild of one that left your meadow for last year's 3000 km (1865 mi.) trip south.

In mid-August, warblers begin their fall migration. If you sit quietly outside, you can watch as the warblers flit through in waves. They don't flock and travel large distances in the daytime. They seem to go tree by tree, feeding and chirping along the way. A field guide to birds will help you identify the warblers, but they aren't called "confusing fall warblers" for nothing! In fall, they all have similar plumage — mostly olive green, white and yellow. Watch carefully for the subtle differences between them — white wing bars, eye patches or yellow throats.

FRISBEE GOLF

Are you ready for the challenge of Frisbee golf? This crazy all-season game borrows from traditional golf, but no golfing experience is required.

GETTING READY

Plan the course with the help of an adult. Try to include a variety of terrains such as a beach, a lawn, hills and rocks. Make sure hazards such as deep water, poison ivy or cliffs are out of bounds. Avoid any neighbors' property — including their prize petunias.

You'll need:
9 Frisbee-sized circles of cardboard
felt markers
tape and thumbtacks
a Frisbee for each player or team
a pencil
paper for scorecards

1.

Label the cardboard circles, or "flags," with the numbers 1 through 9.

2.

Choose a starting line and place the first flag about 25 steps away. Tape or tack the flag about 1 m (3 ft.) above the ground on a tree, a rock or the side of a building. Choose a spot to post the second flag, about 25 steps from the first. Continue until you have placed all nine circles. It's okay if the paths cross one another.

3.
Walk the course to decide on the number of shots each "hole" should take. This is called the par. Easy holes are par 2; more difficult ones, par 3. If a hole is on very difficult terrain and will take several lucky shots to get there, call it a par 4. Mark the par on each flag.

PLAYING THE GAME

- Each player throws the Frisbee from the starting line, trying to strike the first flag. If he misses, he takes his next shot from the place where his Frisbee landed. Count up the number of tosses it takes and record it on your scorecard. Take turns so all players complete each hole before you go on to the next.

- The object of the game is to finish the course with the lowest score. It may take several rounds before you get a good score.

- If it is too difficult to score par on a hole, increase the par. If it is too easy, reduce the par.

MORE

HOW TO THROW A FRISBEE

Grasp the Frisbee by the outside rim, placing your thumb along the edge as shown. Cross your arm over your chest and bend your knees a little. Swing the Frisbee forward, releasing it at hip level as you straighten your legs. Practice until you have perfected the standard Frisbee throw. Soon, you'll be able to control how far you throw the Frisbee and the direction of your throw.

RULES

- If you throw your Frisbee into water, add one penalty shot to your score. Retrieve your Frisbee with an adult watching.

- You're allowed one "Mulligan" per round of nine holes. That means if you make a terrible shot, you can take it again without counting it.

- Don't walk in front of other players while they are taking their turns. If you interfere with a shot, you add one point to your score and the player takes the shot over.

- If the family dog runs off with your Frisbee, mark your spot and chase him. No penalty!

PAR FOR THE PARK

If it's not possible to lay out an organized course, create the game as you play. Take turns deciding which object to aim for next and how many throws are allowed. Keep score in your head.

Hit the fountain in four

ROCK ART

Gather some stones and take a good look at them. You may be able to arrange them together to make an animal or a sculpture. Or maybe one stone in the bunch can be made into something interesting. All over the world, people use ordinary rocks and stones in interesting and artistic ways. Here are some ideas for you to try with your rock collection.

TRAIL SCULPTURES

On hiking trails, people often pile rocks for landmarks and trail guides. These rock piles are called cairns. In some desert areas of the American southwest, people leave a short tower of flat, round rocks on the trailside and then lay a pointed stone on top to indicate the direction to follow. Following a trail marked with

rocks is attractive because it blends so neatly into the surroundings. And it also feels mysterious — where will the wordless directions take you?

In the Arctic, Inuit people have turned trail marking into an art. They construct rock markers to look like giant humans and call them inukshuk,

which means "stone in likeness of a person." Hundreds of years ago, the Inuit marked caribou migration routes with these inukshuk cairns.

Try finding rocks you can pile so they stand together freely but sturdily, show clearly a human form and also indicate a direction. It's not as easy as you think — maybe that's why inukshuks make fascinating sculptures as well as trail markers.

107

21 BASKETBALL

If you have a basketball but no hoops and no team, you can still play a rousing game with a friend and practice your skills.

You'll need:
an old bushel basket, wastebasket or a plastic pail big enough to hold the ball
a saw
a hammer and some nails
a piece of chalk

1.
Find a flat, hard surface, such as a patio or a driveway with a post, pole, deck or wooden fence beside it.

2.
With an adult's help and permission, saw the bottom off your old basket. (This is only necessary if the basket will be placed too high to get the ball out of easily — see next step.)

3.
Ask an adult to tack one side of your basket no more than 3 m (9 ft.) up on the post or the side of the deck or fence.

4.
With the chalk, draw a line on the asphalt about 3 m (9 ft.) away from the basket. This is the free-throw line.

PLAYING THE GAME

To start, the players take turns trying to "break the ice" — that is, sink a basket from the chalk line. Once a player breaks the ice, she can start counting points and gets to shoot again and again from behind the chalk line until she misses the basket, ending her turn.

When the ice-breaker finally misses, the other player runs to get the rebound and tries to break the ice from where he catches it. If he gets a basket, he gets to try a free throw from behind the chalk line and keeps shooting and counting points until he misses. Then the first player runs for the rebound and shoots from where she grabs it.

If either player shoots an air ball — that is, shoots and misses the basket so badly the rim is not even touched — his opponent grabs the "rebound" and walks to anywhere under the basket to take a shot.

SCORING

Players earn one point for breaking the ice, two points for every other free-throw basket from the chalk line, and one point for every basket earned from a rebound. The first player to reach exactly 21 wins. If a player goes over 21, she goes back to zero. This can happen if a player has 20 points and then sinks a free throw.

PEACH BASKETBALL

When Canadian James Naismith invented the game of basketball in 1891, he tacked a peach basket to each end wall of a gymnasium in Massachusetts. Why peach baskets? He grew up on a fruit farm.

JUGGLING

How many objects can you keep in the air at once? One? Two? Juggling isn't as easy as it looks. It takes special training and concentration. Keep your eye on the ball and practice, practice, practice.

Try juggling small beanbags or nonbouncy balls, such as old tennis balls. Whichever you choose, you must be able to hold two in one hand. Start with one ball and work your way up to two or three.

JUGGLE ONE

1.
Hold one ball in your "comfy" hand, or dominant hand. Throw the ball up in an arch and catch it with your other hand. Pass the ball back to your comfy hand and repeat, over and over again.

2.
Now reverse the direction of the ball, throwing from your other hand to your comfy hand. It will take longer to perfect this move.

JUGGLE TWO

1.
When you feel ready, move on to two balls. Hold one ball in the fingertips of each hand. Toss the ball from your comfy hand up in an arch toward your other hand. When this ball reaches the top of the arch, toss the ball from your other hand toward your comfy hand, below the arch of the first ball. Catch the balls. Practice this move.

2.
Talk to yourself and get a rhythm going in your head. Saying "one, two; one, two; one, two" will help.

3.
Now practice the reverse motion, throwing from your other hand first. Keep doing this continuous motion until you've perfected it. You'll be chasing balls until you get the hang of it.

JUGGLE THREE

1.
To add a third ball, place two in the comfy hand and one in the other. Toss one ball from your comfy hand in a high arch toward the other hand. When the ball is at the top of the arch, throw the ball from the other hand back toward the comfy hand. When that ball is at the top and starting to come down, toss the third ball. Catch all the balls. Now you should have two balls in your other hand and one in your comfy hand. Return one to your comfy hand and repeat.

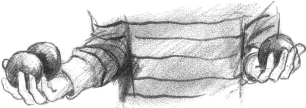

2.
Continue practicing. Once you have perfected this move, try to keep the three balls in the air in continuous motion. Say "one, two, three" over and over to yourself.

Now you know what someone means when she says, "I have three balls in the air" — she's busy!

MARBLES

When you play marbles, you "play for keeps." That's marble talk for winning any marble you hit — and losing your own when you miss. So, if you don't want to lose your marbles, practice these games first alone or with a friend. Head for a patch of smooth, hard dirt.

HOW TO SHOOT A MARBLE

1.
Kneel on one or both knees.

2.
Turn your hand on its side and touch the ground with at least one knuckle.

3.
Curl your index finger and balance the shooter in the curl.

4.
Brace your thumb behind the shooter, aim and then flick the shooter with your thumb, keeping the rest of your hand still.

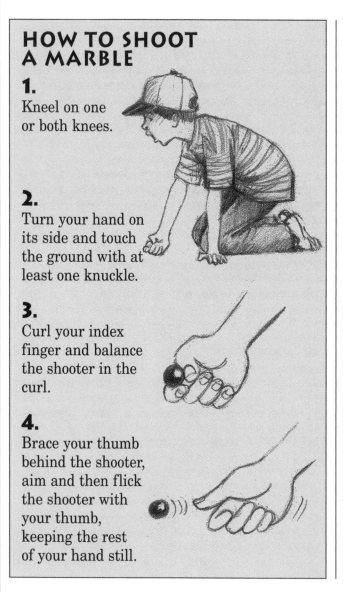

RINGER

Draw a circle about 1 m (3 ft.) in diameter in the dirt. Each player places an equal number of marbles inside the ring.

Players take turns shooting at the marbles from outside the ring. If you knock a marble out of the ring, you keep it and shoot again from where your shooter stopped. Your turn ends when you fail to knock any marbles out or your shooter stops inside the ring. Any shooters inside the ring remain there for others to shoot at. The game ends when all the marbles have been shot out of the circle.

CASTLES

Two players kneel facing each other, at least 1 m (3 ft.) apart. Each player builds a castle of four marbles — three on the bottom touching one another and one balanced on top. Both players take turns shooting at each other's castles. If one person knocks down the other's castle, that person gets to take all four castle marbles. Castle owners may keep any shooters that miss their castle. The game ends when one player has had enough.

SPANNIES

Draw a shooting line in the dirt. The first player, or the starter, rolls a marble from the shooting line. This is the target marble. The other player tries to hit that marble from the shooting line with four marbles — or some other number agreed upon at the start.

The starter wins any marble that does not hit or fall within a span of the target marble. A span is the distance from the end of the starter's thumb to the tip of his index finger. If the shooter's marble hits the target marble or comes within a span of it, she gets the target marble and her shooter. The starter then rolls a new target marble. The game is over when both players have had an equal number of turns being the starter.

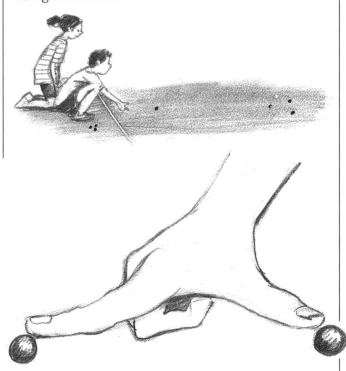

HIDING GAMES

Hiding outdoors provides the perfect opportunity for daydreaming or watching the natural world around you. But keep your wits about you so you'll be ready for the dash to home base.

HIDE-AND-SEEK

1.
Choose a home base — a tree or a back step is perfect.

2.
One person is It. The other players hide. If you're hiding, choose a spot where you will be safe and well camouflaged. It's best if you can see home base.

3.
It covers his eyes and counts loudly and slowly. When he reaches 25, he shouts, "Ready or not, here I come," and the search is on.

4.
When It sees someone, he shouts that player's name: "One, two, three on Madeline!" and they both race back to home base. If It wins the race, the caught player must help find the others. If the caught player reaches home base first, she is "home free" and doesn't help look for the others.

5.
The game is over when every person has been found. The one who was caught first is It for the next game.

HIDE AND SQUISH

One person hides in a snug spot, such as a garden shed, behind a woodpile, or under a low-branched tree, while the others count out loud to 25. The players split up to look for the hidden player. As each person finds the hiding spot, she quietly climbs in. When all the players are squished in, the game is over. The first person to find the hiding spot starts the next squish.

WINTER HIDEOUTS

In northern climates, many species of snakes have "squishes" of their own. They hibernate in groups, choosing protected places such as rock gardens, rotting stumps and old wells. Canada is home to the world's largest snake squish. More than 10 000 red-sided garter snakes snuggle closely together in Manitoba's underground caverns from September until April.

CAPTURE THE FLAG

There are flags on top of mountains and on the Moon. They flutter back and forth proclaiming, "We did it, we were here!" Capture the flag is a game of speed, strategy and patience. Be prepared to stand guard for your flag or risk prison to snatch your opponents'. Set up generous but safe boundaries, choose two teams of at least three people, find or make a flag for each team, and you're ready for action.

PLAYING THE GAME

Capture the flag can be played on a playing field or a beach, or in a park or a large garden. Use a garden hose or rope to divide the play area in half. Mark a line 1 m (3 ft.) on each side. The space between these two lines is the safe zone.

1.

Each team chooses a tree branch or pole on which to fly its flag. The flag must be visible.

2.

The object of the game is to find and capture the flag of the opposing team and return it to your territory, without being touched. At the same time, each team tries to protect its own flag.

3.

If a player crosses into the opponents' territory and is touched by a player on that team, he becomes a prisoner and must sit near the opponents' flag. A teammate can free prisoners by sneaking in and touching them. The rescuer and rescued players must return to their own side before attempting to capture the flag.

4.

Work as a team with a plan of attack. Leave at least one player guarding your own flag. Distract your opponents with loud noises or by running in a zigzag manner. When they're off guard, race in and snatch their flag. Be ready to sprint back to the safe zone if you're spotted.

5.

The team whose players capture the opponents' flag and safely return with it to their own territory, wins.

TIPS

- In defending the flag or in trying to capture your opponents' flag, be sneaky. It is best not to be seen.

- It is hard to defend your flag and win this game if your teammates are captured. Rescue them first; snatch the flag later.

- If you are playing with a large group, members of one team should wear something to identify them, such as a bandanna or hat.

FLAG SIGNALS

For more than 5000 years, people have used flags to send messages. Flags can signal retreat, surrender or charge, friend or foe, good news or bad, keep out, or quarantine.

If capture the flag has gone on for hours and you are ready for lunch, wave a white flag. It's the international signal for a truce.

COMET BALL

Make a comet ball and leave your old games of catch in the dust — intergalactic dust, that is. With a comet ball, you can double both the speed and the distance of your throws. Just be careful you don't throw your comet ball so high it gets caught in the top of a tall tree or breaks a neighbor's window.

You'll need:

a discarded pair of nylon stockings

scissors

an old tennis ball or a rubber ball

1.
Cut off one whole stocking leg with your scissors.

2.
Stuff the ball into the toe of the cutoff stocking leg.

3.
Tie a knot at the heel of the stocking so the ball won't work its way back down the leg.

4.
Find a big, open, outdoor space and practice throwing your comet ball. Hold it by the leg of the stocking and swing it around and around, then let it go. To catch the comet ball, grab for the tail (the leg of the stocking) as it flies by.

118

PLAYING WITH THE COMET BALL

Try playing throw and catch games, but stand far apart. Or line up and see who can throw the comet ball the farthest.

Adapt strategies for monkey in the middle. In the regular game, two players throw a ball back and forth, and a third player in the middle tries to catch it. With a comet ball, the ball will sail way over your head if you are in the middle. You have to move so you're nearly at one end or the other to have any chance of catching it. When the middle person catches the ball, he switches places with the player who threw it.

COMETS AND METEORS

Comets are clouds of frozen gas and dust particles left over from the birth of our solar system. They travel in long orbits or trails. When a comet nears the Sun, part of its icy coating melts and some dust particles fall off along the trail. The warming gases reflect sunlight, so the comet seems to grow a large head and tail.

Bright comets are seen only three or four times in a hundred years. But you can see meteor showers each year in the fall — October 19–24, November 16 and December 10–14. Meteors actually begin as dust particles left along an old comet trail. The particles hit the edge of Earth's atmosphere and flash as they vaporize on contact. Each fall, Earth passes across three ancient comet trails and we are rewarded with meteor showers, or shooting stars, each of those nights.

CROKINOLE

Can you dodge obstacles, scatter opponents and hit the winning jackpot with only the flick of a finger? Test your skills in the crazy game of crokinole. You can even make your own crokinole board.

You'll need:
four 75 cm (30 in.) squares of sturdy cardboard
a 30 cm (1 ft.) length of string attached to a pencil
scissors or a craft knife
a measuring tape
12 checker disks of one color and 12 of another
white glue
a black marker
8 sturdy thumbtacks

1.

Cut the corners off one square of cardboard to make an eight-sided figure. This will be your crokinole board base.

2.

With your thumb, hold the end of the string on the midpoint of a second cardboard square. Pull the pencil so the string is tight and draw a circle with a radius of the full 30 cm (1 ft.) of the string.

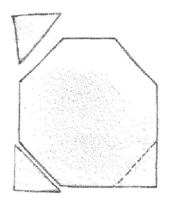

3.

Cut out the circle and then cut two more from the remaining cardboard pieces.

4.

Cut a hole, just larger than a checker disk, in the center of the three cardboard circles.

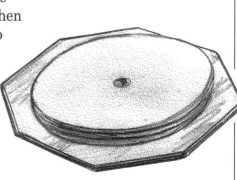

5.

Glue the circles together and then glue them onto the middle of your base piece. Weigh down the board with a heavy object while the glue dries.

6.

Draw three more circles with the string and pencil on the top piece of cardboard from the midpoint. The radius of the first circle should be 28 cm ($11\frac{1}{2}$ in.), the second 20 cm (8 in.), and the third 10 cm (4 in.). Go over the lines with marker.

7.

Place the eight tacks evenly around the smallest drawn circle.

8.

With the marker, write the number 20 in the hole, 15 in the ring between the hole and the tacks, 10 outside the tacks and 5 in the outside ring.

9.

The outside line is the starting line. Draw four evenly spaced lines from it, across the ring valued 5, to the next line. These are called quadrant lines.

CROKINOLE RULES

With two players, each starts with 12 checker disks of one color. Players sit opposite each other and take turns shooting their disks.

- Place a disk on the starting line inside the quadrant facing you. Hold your middle finger under your thumb and flick it to shoot the disk forward. Once the game starts, players cannot change places or move the board.

- The object of the game is to shoot your disks into high-scoring positions and knock your opponent's disks into low-scoring ones or out altogether. When a disk lands in the hole, it is removed but counts as 20.

- At the end of each round, players add up their scores. Disks touching lines take the lower value. Disks on the starting line are out. Rounds are played until a player reaches 100 points.

- With four players, each starts with six checkers. Make two teams with team members facing one another. Play moves clockwise around the table.

PICKUP STICKS

How steady is your hand? How sharp is your eye? Make a set of pickup sticks and challenge one or two friends to test their skills.

You'll need:
20 straight, narrow sticks with the bark peeled off, about 12 cm (4½ in.) long. Trimmed wooden barbecue skewers will also do.
acrylic paints (black, green, orange and yellow)
a paintbrush
water for cleaning the brush

- Paint both ends of one stick black.

- Paint both ends of three sticks green.

- Paint both ends of six sticks orange.

- Paint both ends of ten sticks yellow.

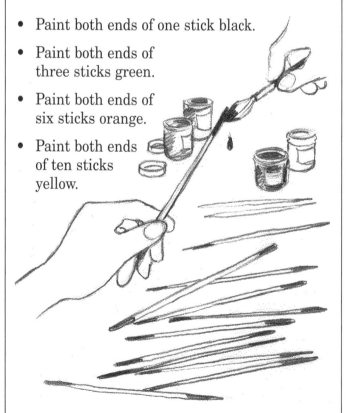

PLAYING THE GAME

1.
Gather up all the sticks except the black one and hold them in a bunch. Insert the black stick into the center.

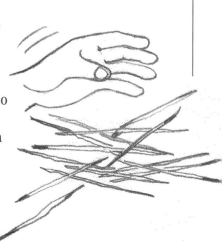

2.
Hold the sticks with one hand so that one end of the bunch touches the floor. Open your hand and pull it back quickly so the sticks topple on top of one another on the floor.

3.

Players take turns trying to pick up one stick at a time, using only their fingers and without moving any other stick.

4.

If a player picks up one stick and the others do not move, she sets the stick aside and gets another turn. The player continues as long as she is successful.

5.

If someone, in trying to pick up a stick, wiggles another, she leaves both sticks where they lie and her turn is over.

6.

The person who successfully retrieves the black stick can use it as a tool to help retrieve other sticks. The black stick is better than your finger for flicking sticks off the top of the pile or for pulling back a stick that is touching others. You still cannot wiggle others when using the black stick.

SCORING

When all the sticks have been picked up, players count their score.

- The black stick is worth 4 points.

- Each green stick is worth 3 points.

- Each orange stick is worth 2 points.

- Each yellow stick is worth 1 point.

MARATHON CARD GAMES

Snap and war are two card games that can last for hours. You'll need quick reflexes and plenty of time to win.

♠ ♥ ♦ ♣ ♠ ♥ ♦ ♣ ♠ ♥ ♦ ♣ ♠ ♥ ♦ ♣ ♠ ♥ ♦ ♣ ♠ | ♣ ♠ ♥ ♦ ♣ ♠

SNAP

Have you got a drawer full of old cards — two or more decks with a few cards missing from each? Mix them together to make the perfect snap deck. Now all you need is one friend and a place where you can make lots of noise.

PLAYING THE GAME

1.
Players sit opposite each other. One person deals out all the cards, facedown, into two draw piles, one in front of each player.

2.
Ready, set, go. Players turn over one card each at the same time and place it faceup in a pile beside their draw pile.

3.
This is repeated until the two cards are of the same value. The first person to yell, "Snap!" wins all the faceup cards. These are placed facedown at the bottom of her draw pile.

4.
Play resumes as before. When all the cards in a player's draw pile have been turned faceup, the player leaves the top card faceup on the table and turns the rest of the cards over, making a new draw pile. The game continues until one person has all the cards.

ANIMAL SNAP

Crank up the noise level of this already raucous game by assigning each player an animal such as a pig, dog or cow. Instead of saying "snap," players must make the appropriate noise — grunt, bark, moo and so on. The first player to make her noise gets all the faceup cards. If a player gets mixed up and makes the wrong animal noise or says "snap," he loses all the cards in his faceup pile.

♠ ♥ ♦ ♣ ♠ ♥ ♦ ♣ ♠ ♥ ♦ ♣ ♠ ♥ ♦ ♣ ♠ ♥ ♦ ♣ ♠ ♥ ♦ ♣ ♠ ♥

WAR

There's no shooting or prisoners in this game of war — only two friends trying to win all the cards.

PLAYING THE GAME

1.

Players sit opposite each other. One person deals out a complete deck of 52 cards into two piles facedown on the table.

2.

Cards are valued in order, with 2 carrying the lowest value and ace the highest. All suits are equal.

3.

At the same time, each player turns over the top card on his pile. The person with the highest card wins both cards and sets them aside, facedown in a winnings pile.

4.

Players continue as above until the two upturned cards are of the same value. War is now declared. Each player draws the next three cards from the top of his pile and places them facedown on the table. The fourth card is drawn and turned faceup. The highest card wins both piles of five. If the cards are the same again, the process is repeated until one card is higher. The winner takes all the cards used in this war.

5.

When all the cards in the draw piles have been won or lost, players shuffle their winnings piles and keep playing. The game continues until one person has won all the cards.

125

SKILLFUL STUNTS

What can you do with a coin, a spoon and a lazy afternoon? Practice these simple stunts and dazzle your family with a display of your craft by dinnertime. This may be the beginning of a promising career or just a fun way to pass the afternoon.

MATHEMAGICAL SPOONS

Two spoons and a pair of hands is all it takes to make math magic.

1.
Sit on the ground or at a table and ask your family or friends to gather 'round. Explain that you will be demonstrating a number with your magic spoons. Their job is to guess the number and say it aloud, but not say how they got the number.

2.
Lay the spoons on the ground in a random pattern. Tell your audience that the spoons are showing a number between one and ten.

3.
Rest your hands on either side of the spoons, with some fingers folded under and some lying flat. The number of visible fingers indicates the magic number.

4.
If no one guesses, reveal the number and repeat the trick, showing a different number. Eventually, someone will catch on and become your assistant. Keep going until everyone has figured out the trick. Don't be surprised if a younger sibling or friend wants to demonstrate the trick next. Play along, even though you've got his number.

DISAPPEARING COINS

Where did that quarter go? How did it vanish into your arm and reappear somewhere else? Keep your friends guessing with this trick — your success will depend on how quickly you can maneuver. Remember, the hand is quicker than the eye.

1.
Sit with your left elbow on a table and your left hand resting nonchalantly on your shoulder.

2.
With a dramatic flourish, pick up a coin with your right hand. Explain to your audience that you will make the coin disappear into your left forearm and reappear somewhere else on your body.

3.
Rub the coin on your left arm. Appear to be serious and concentrating.

4.
Drop the coin and quickly put both hands on the table. Pretend to retrieve the coin with your right hand as you secretly pick it up with your left hand. Place the coin on your shoulder while continuing to rub your forearm with your right hand.

5.
After several seconds, open your right hand and exclaim that the coin has vanished. Pick it off your left shoulder and show the amazed crowd.

WHAT TO LOOK FOR IN THE AUTUMN SKY

Get acquainted with the constellation Cassiopeia, the Queen, and she'll lead you to most of the famous stars and constellations in the autumn sky. You can see Cassiopeia all year round, but in autumn, she takes center stage.

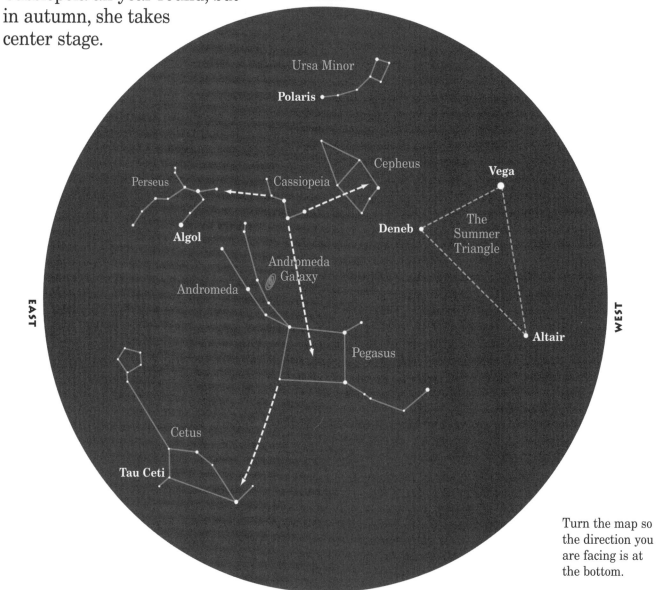

Turn the map so the direction you are facing is at the bottom.

CASSIOPEIA, THE QUEEN

To find Cassiopeia in the fall, face north. This circumpolar constellation looks like an M or a W. The Summer Triangle lies to the west of Cassiopeia; Ursa Minor, the Little Dipper, farther north; and the Milky Way stretches east–west across the sky in a band that goes through Cassiopeia.

Cassiopeia

PERSEUS, THE HERO

Follow the Milky Way east from Cassiopeia to find Perseus. Algol, the most southwesterly star in Perseus, is actually a double star — two close stars that circle and eclipse each other every three days.

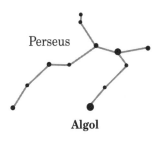

Perseus

Algol

CEPHEUS, THE KING

West of Cassiopeia, you'll see a group of stars that looks like a house. As night deepens, Cepheus, the King, leads Cassiopeia, his Queen, across the sky.

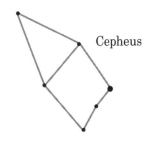

Cepheus

PEGASUS, THE WINGED HORSE

Look for four stars in a square south of Cassiopeia. This is the Great Square of Pegasus, the body of the horse. When you look through the square, you are looking beyond the Milky Way Galaxy.

THE ANDROMEDA GALAXY

Our nearest galaxy neighbor lies between Cassiopeia and Pegasus. It looks like a hazy smudge in the sky. The Andromeda Galaxy is a spiral galaxy like our own, but it's larger. The constellation Andromeda, the Princess, lies below the galaxy in a V of stars that starts at one corner of the Great Square of Pegasus.

CETUS, THE WHALE

South of Andromeda, near the southern horizon, look for the monstrous whale. Scientists think one of the fainter stars in Cetus, Tau Ceti, is so similar to our Sun that it's a good place to begin a search for extraterrestrial life!

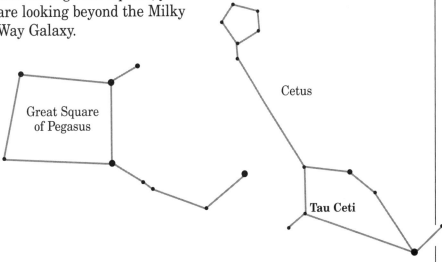

Great Square of Pegasus

Cetus

Tau Ceti

THE NORTHERN LIGHTS

On crisp, clear nights in fall or winter, keep your eyes on the northern sky. If you notice a greenish glow, you may be in for a display of northern lights.

WHAT CAUSES THE NORTHERN LIGHTS?

Electrically charged particles constantly stream toward Earth from the Sun in the solar wind. Earth's magnetic field deflects most of these particles back out into space. But some particles slip through the magnetic field, escape, dive toward Earth and enter our atmosphere near the North and South Poles.

When these particles strike air molecules, faint jolts of light energy are released. When sunspots form on the Sun, more electrically charged particles flood into our atmosphere and more collisions occur, and the northern lights grow bigger and clearer.

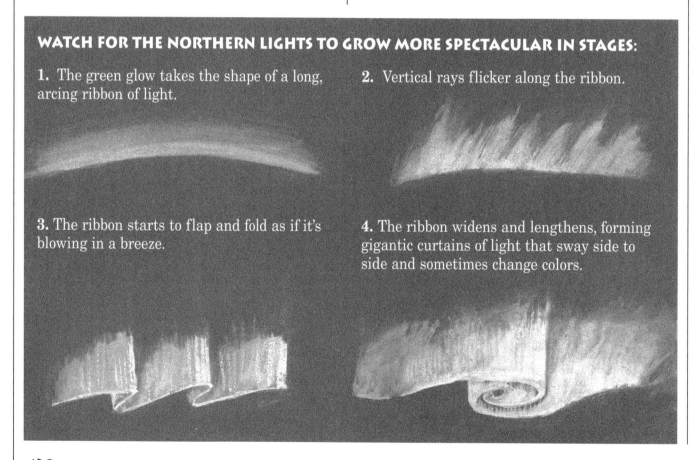

WATCH FOR THE NORTHERN LIGHTS TO GROW MORE SPECTACULAR IN STAGES:

1. The green glow takes the shape of a long, arcing ribbon of light.

2. Vertical rays flicker along the ribbon.

3. The ribbon starts to flap and fold as if it's blowing in a breeze.

4. The ribbon widens and lengthens, forming gigantic curtains of light that sway side to side and sometimes change colors.

OLD EXPLANATIONS FOR THE NORTHERN LIGHTS

- In stories told by Inuit elders, the northern lights are spirits playing football in the sky. The players use a walrus skull for the ball.

- In Maine and New Brunswick, Passamaquoddy elders tell of a game of lacrosse in the land of the northern lights. The players wear lights on their heads and rainbows around their waists.

- To some Siberians, the northern lights are ghost warriors replaying old battles in heaven.

- For the Saami of northern Europe, the northern lights are spirits of the dead lighting up the sky with a message of hope — spring will come again.

- The Shetland Islanders of northern Scotland call the northern lights "the merry dancers."

131

LITTLE DIPPER STORIES

The Big Dipper outshines the Little Dipper. But during autumn evenings, the Little Dipper (Ursa Minor, the Little Bear) is higher in the sky and easier to see than the Big Dipper. The Little Dipper shares most stories with the Big Dipper, but these are a few of its own.

The famous sixteenth-century German mapmaker of the cosmos, Petrus Apianus, didn't see a bear in the Little Dipper. He thought these seven stars were the nymph daughters of Atlas, the great Titan. They lived on Mount Atlas, where they grew and tended the tree of the golden apples. Mother Earth gave this tree to Zeus when he married. The apples were the fruit of everlasting life, and only gods were allowed to pick them.

Egyptian skywatchers saw a giant hippopotamus in the Little Dipper. Because the northern stars never set, the Egyptians were superstitious about them and thought they might be evil. It was the strong hippo's job to circle the North Pole and keep order among the other circumpolar stars. As well, the hippo gobbled up all dead people who had lived wicked lives.

YOU NAME IT!

The Little Dipper has been called many names over the millennia. Which do you like best?

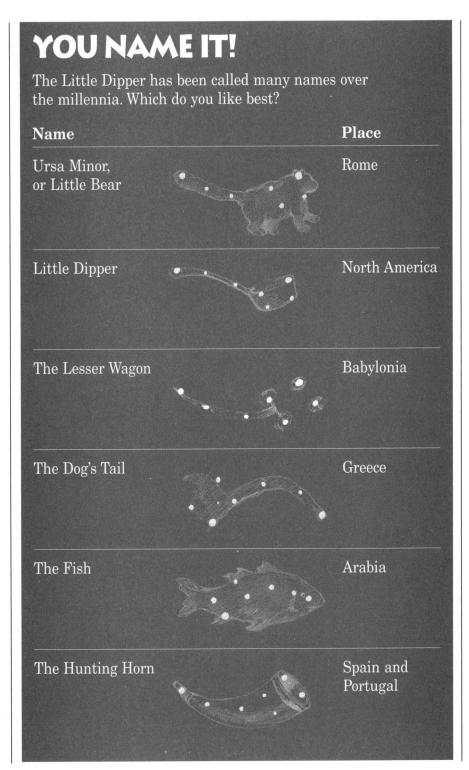

Name		Place
Ursa Minor, or Little Bear		Rome
Little Dipper		North America
The Lesser Wagon		Babylonia
The Dog's Tail		Greece
The Fish		Arabia
The Hunting Horn		Spain and Portugal

DIPPERS FLYING HIGH

In 1926, Alaska had a contest to decide the design for its state flag. A thirteen-year-old boy named Benny Benson combined the stars of the Big Dipper and the Pole Star in the Little Dipper on a dark blue background. This flag has been waving over Alaska ever since.

❄ WINTER ❄

Winter has arrived: snow, ice, wind …
and fun! Snow makes it easy to find out
what your local wildlife has been up to —
learn how to spot tracks and figure out who
they belong to. You can also get to know your
local winter birds by feeding them their
favorite food. Winter time is a great time to get
outside: learn traditional snow games; make a
rink for skating, sliding and shinny; build a
snowman or two; or even have your own
winter Olympics! And when the winds howl
and the snow is coming down, you can be cozy
inside making some wintery crafts.

WINTER SUN

Early arctic people invented snow goggles to protect their eyes from the intense glare of the sun bouncing off snow. Make your own snow goggles and see what a difference they make.

You'll need:
scissors or a craft knife
a cardboard egg carton
2 pieces of string, each 50 cm (20 in.) long

1.

Cut two cups from the egg carton so that they are attached to each other and to the flaps of cardboard on the outer side of each cup.

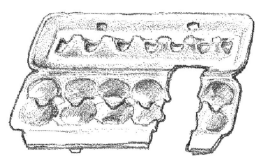

2.

Trim the cardboard bridge between the two cups until the goggles fit comfortably against your nose and brow.

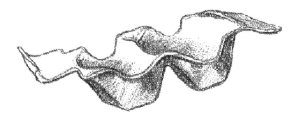

3.

Cut a 0.5 cm ($\frac{1}{4}$ in.) slit across the bottom and a little way up the sides of each cup. Place the goggles on your eyes and decide if you need to widen or lengthen the slits so that you can see well straight ahead and side to side.

4.

Poke a hole in each side flap and attach the strings so you can tie on the goggles at the back of your head.

5.

On a sunny day, test your goggles. Don't wear them near traffic or in places where you need to take care as you walk or climb. **Never stare right at the sun.**

THE SUN'S SPECIAL EFFECTS

The North Pole tilts away from the sun in winter. That makes winter days north of the Equator shorter. Sunshine that does reach the north comes in at an angle, from the southern sky. With fewer hours of sun and with less direct sun, northern lands cool down. But winter sun, because it is weaker and shining from afar, can make amazing special effects in the skies. Look for sun dogs, sun haloes and sun pillars.

Sun dogs appear when the sun is low in the sky. They look like mini-suns that sit beside the sun. A sun dog is an image of the sun made by ice crystals in the air. When two sun dogs line up on either side of the sun, a sun halo may connect them to a huge arcing circle over the sun. A sun pillar is a beam of light that shines up from the rising or setting sun like a giant searchlight. The sun's rays have to hit six-sided ice crystals in a certain way to make this effect.

SNOW SCIENCE

What is freezing cold but makes a warm blanket? What grows on dirt but is sparkling clean? Snow, of course! Fill a measuring cup with a handful of fresh snow. Let the snow melt and take a look.

- You'll see there's much less water in the cup than there was snow. That's because snow is filled with tiny air pockets. When the snow melts, the air escapes. The air pockets in snow act as insulation so that animals and people can live in snow houses and keep warm.

- At the bottom of the cup, you'll see specks of dirt. That's because snowflakes form when snow crystals collect on airborne dust and dirt particles. The crystals actually grow on the dirt. When snow melts, the dirt is left behind.

138

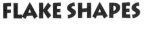

SNOWFLAKE IMPRESSIONS

See just how intricate newly fallen snowflakes can be.

You'll need:
hairspray (CFC-free)
a small pane of glass
a magnifying glass

1.
Spray one side of the pane of glass with hairspray and place it in the freezer.

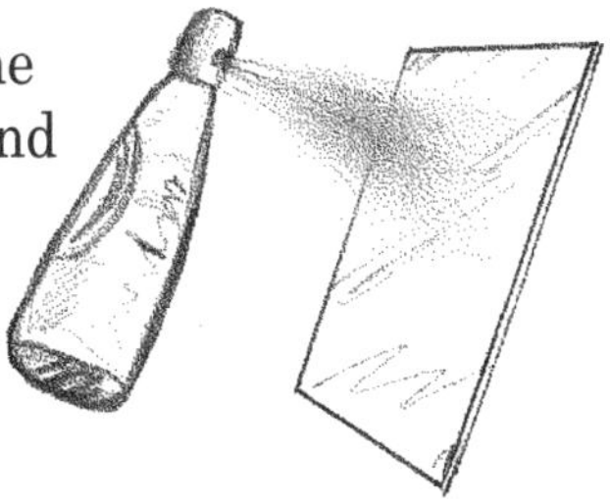

2.
When it snows, carefully carry the pane outside with the hairspray side up and let a few snowflakes fall on it. Look at them with the magnifying glass.

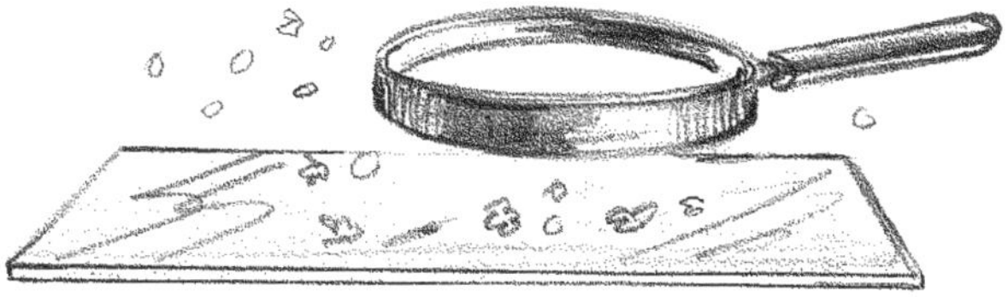

3.
Carefully take the pane inside and let the snowflakes melt. Use your magnifying glass to look at the impressions left on the pane.

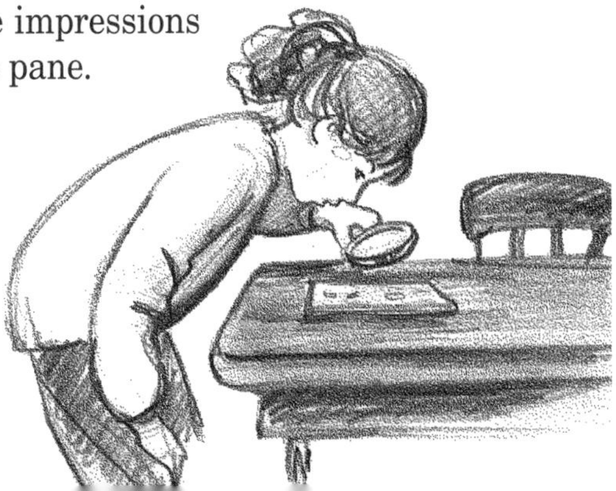

FLAKE SHAPES

No one has ever found two snowflakes that are exactly the same — but most are six sided. Each snowflake is made up of snow crystals — very large flakes may contain up to 200 crystals. Look for these snowflake shapes in fresh snow:

- hexagonal prisms

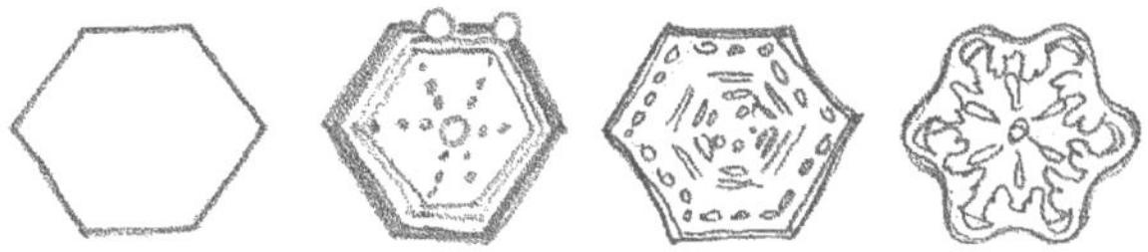

- stellar crystals

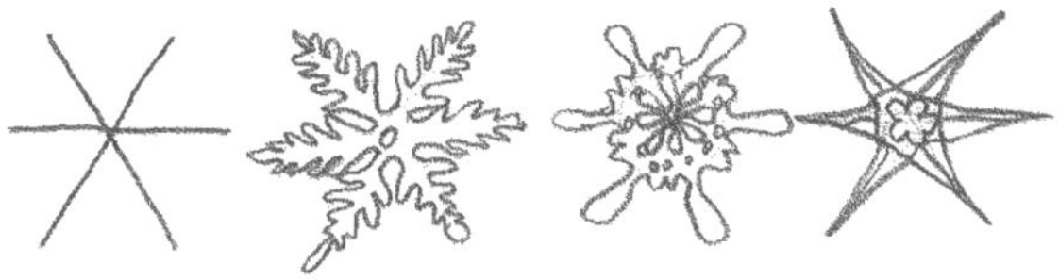

- hexagonal columns

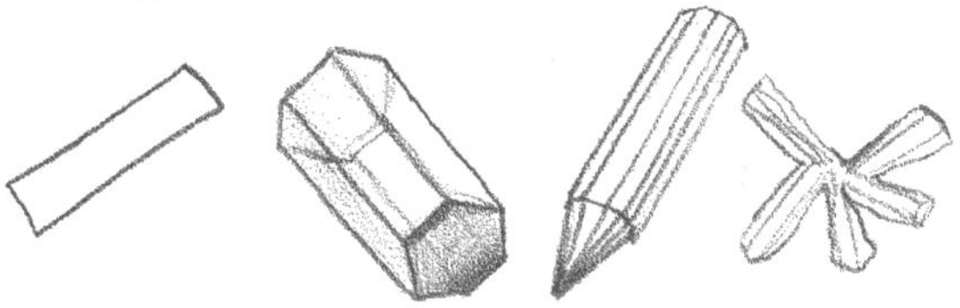

- needles

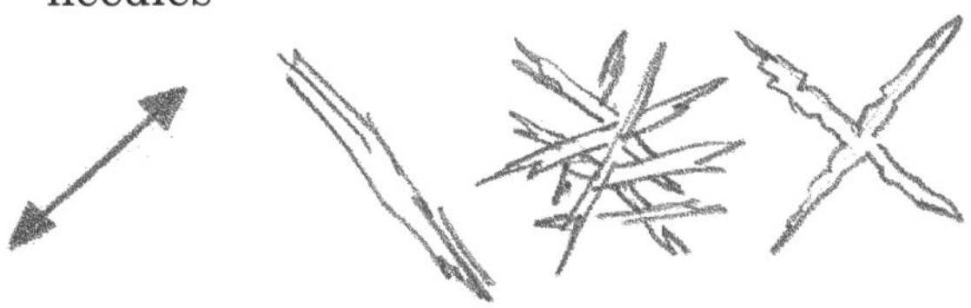

- spatial dendrites

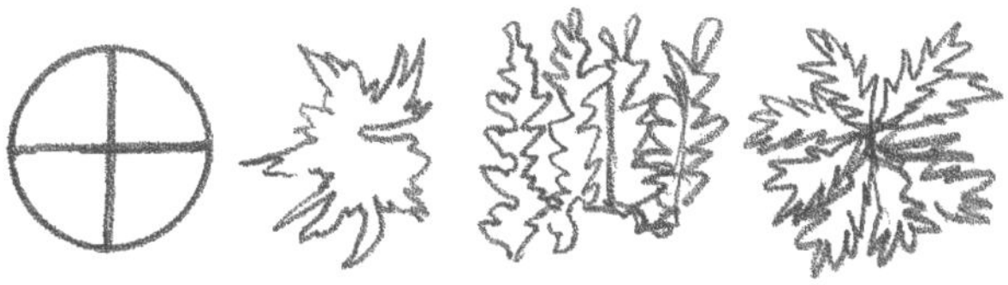

MAKING TRACKS

When the ground is covered with snow, food is scarce and many creatures are hibernating. Animal sightings are rare. But there are often signs of nocturnal or secretive visitors. Learn to identify snow prints. Can you tell if the animal was sauntering along, running or being chased? Then check some trees for animal signs.

deer

lynx

house cat

dog

coyote

rabbit

squirrel

porcupine

mouse

weasel

raccoon

dove

sparrow

crow

140

A TREE TELLS A TALE

A tightly packed leaf and twig nest as big as a bicycle tire is usually the summer home to squirrels. They often winter inside hollow tree limbs lined with leaves and moss.

Wood chips at the base and a gaping hole in the trunk mean a woodpecker has been spearing insect larvae with its long tongue or building a nest.

Snowshoe hares gnaw small bites from the bark of woody plants.

Discarded pinecones that are picked clean of seeds mean a red squirrel lives nearby.

If large pieces of bark, entire twigs and succulent buds have been chiseled from a tree, a porcupine has dined.

Missing bark and gouged wood ribbed with teeth marks tell you a hungry moose has made a meal of a young tree.

Deep claw marks on tree trunks are a black bear's way of saying "I'm big and I'm nearby." It could be hibernating under that tree!

Pooplike pellets at the base of a tree may mean a great horned owl is roosting there. They eat small animals and birds whole and then regurgitate — spit out — fuzzy pellets of indigestible feathers, bones and fur.

141

UNDER THE SNOW

When you walk with a dog through freshly fallen snow, does it burrow its nose in for a sniff? Did you know that it smells mice, voles, weasels and other creatures that live under the blanket of snow?

ATTRACTING WILDLIFE

To find out what's active under the snow, lure creatures to the surface with a little food. Place some birdseed or bread crumbs beside a sheltered spot, such as a low bush, where you have a good view from a window. On warm days, chipmunks, mice, red squirrels and voles will pack their cheek pouches with food and scurry below the snow again.

TERROR OF THE SNOWBANK

Deep snow protects many creatures from weather, but it doesn't stop predators from stalking them for food. The fierce weasel tunnels under the snow, stunning mice or other small rodents with a high-pitched screech. A lunge to the throat finishes the kill. After devouring the prey, the weasel can move in, taking over its victim's burrow. They insulate their homes with fur plucked from their prey.

Many carnivores that live above the snow — fox, coyote, wolves, lynx, bobcats and wolverines — can smell a meal under the snow. They try to scare out their prey by jumping on top of the burrows or by digging into the snow.

142

TRAILS OF SPRING

In a meadow, the last snow to melt in the spring is under the hard-packed tunnels used by creatures under the snow. If you look closely, you'll find that the tunnels lead to the remains of winter burrows. Look for milkweed fluff, tufts of fur, dried grasses, droppings and footprints in the mud. Turn to page 140 to identify the footprints of the creature that wintered there.

CAMOUFLAGE

Some predators, such as weasels and arctic fox, change color in winter so they can sneak up on their prey unseen. Prey species, such as snowshoe hares or ptarmigan, turn white, making it harder for them to be seen.

WINTER BIRD FEEDING

Get to know the winter birds in your area by feeding them. If you offer a variety of foods, you'll attract and get to know different species.

SITING BIRD FEEDERS

Birds need to feel safe when feeding. Place feeders at least 3 m (10 ft.) from a window and where there is shelter. Make sure the feeder is out of reach of any dogs or cats.

BELL FEEDER

Keep a ready supply of these bell feeders in the freezer. It's time to put out a new one when a squirrel runs away with the walnut.

You'll need:
50 mL (¼ c.) peanut butter
50 mL (¼ c.) lard or bacon drippings
50 mL (¼ c.) sunflower seeds
50 mL (¼ c.) mixed birdseed
a large bowl
a wooden spoon
a clean tin can
string
scissors
a walnut in the shell
a can opener

1.
Combine the peanut butter, lard or bacon drippings, sunflower seeds and birdseed in a large bowl with a wooden spoon. Place one spoonful in the bottom of the can.

2.
Cut a piece of string about 60 cm (2 ft.) long. Tie the string around the walnut and wedge the nut in the middle of the peanut butter mixture in the bottom of the can.

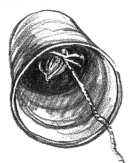

3.
Fill the can with the rest of the mixture, gently pulling the string up through the middle of the can as you fill it. Pat the mixture down with a spoon.

4.
Place the can in the freezer for several hours until the mixture is very hard.

5.
With an adult's help open the bottom of the can with the can opener and carefully discard the lid. Push the frozen contents out of the can, being careful not to cut yourself on the can.

6.
Hang your bell feeder outdoors on a cold day from a tree branch, fence post or a bird feeder. If the weather turns mild, the mixture may fall to the ground where ground-feeding birds will find it.

SUET FEEDER

Many birds need fat in their winter diet to help keep them warm. Ask the butcher at the store for a large piece of beef suet. Place it in an onion bag, tying the bag closed with string or a twist tie. Hang it outside and watch for woodpeckers, chickadees, nuthatches and other hungry birds.

CRASHES

Birds sometimes crash into windows, recover and fly away. To help prevent this, make a black silhouette cutout of a hawk using construction paper or shelf liner and stick it to one corner of the window.

FUN IN THE SNOW

Snow is the main ingredient in all these outdoor games and activities.

SNOW SOCCER

Set the boundaries of the soccer pitch. A rectangular space is ideal but not necessary. Declare trees, rocks, buildings and hazards out of bounds. Set up a goal about 2 m (6½ ft.) wide at either end of the soccer pitch. Players should wear treaded winter boots and layers of clothing, including a hat, gloves and warm pants.

1.

Divide into two teams of three or four players each. Teams choose one defense player and the rest are forwards. It's too cold for a goalie.

2.

The ball is placed in the center of the pitch. With the ball between them, one player from each team faces each other. At the count of three, they try to gain possession of the ball using feet, knees and heads, but no hands.

3.

Players try to kick the ball into the goal of the opposite team. Each goal counts for one point.

4.

When one team hits the ball out of bounds, a member of the other team throws the ball back into play.

5.

When the teams are worn out and ready for a cup of hot chocolate, one player calls, "last goal wins!"

146

TARGET PRACTICE

Using a snowball, pack a snow bull's-eye ring on the side of a tree or a brick wall with no windows. The snow will catch in the rough surface and be easy to see. Take turns aiming for the target. Who can hit the target most often?

> Throwing snowballs is irresistible, but never throw them at people, pets or vehicles. Stick to target practice!

SAY IT WITH SNOW

Spell out a short and simple message, such as "Happy Birthday, Dad" or "Happy Holidays" using a water bottle filled with water and food coloring. If the temperature is below freezing, the message will be visible until the next snowfall.

HOPSCOTCH IN THE SNOW

Use a water bottle filled with water and food coloring to outline a hopscotch board on the snow. Throw a snowball into the first square, hop over it, then hop into every square up to number

10. On the way back, stop to pick up your snowball. Now toss the snowball into number two. You're out if you step on the colored lines or in a square containing another player's snowball.

147

TRADITIONAL SNOW GAMES

The first people of North America played games that combined fun with hunting practice. Play these Native outdoor winter games and increase your ability to throw with power, speed and accuracy.

SNOW SNAKE

The object of snow snake is to throw bone darts to see whose travels farthest along an ice run.

You'll need:
fine sandpaper
a clean pork or beef rib bone or a smooth 15 cm (6 in.) stick
a hand drill with a fine bit
2 feathers or evergreen pieces, each about 4 times as long as the bone
white glue
a shovel

1.
With the sandpaper, smooth the sides of the bone.

2.
Ask an adult to drill a hole in one end of the bone.

3.
Put glue on the shaft end of the feathers (or evergreen) and insert into the hole at the end of the bone.

4.
Shovel a straight stretch of ice or pack down and water a long trench of snow to make a narrow ice run.

5.
Throw the bone dart overhand or sidearm along the run. Draw lines or sprinkle colored drink crystals in the snow to show where each player's dart stops.

6.
For variation, construct a snow ramp along the run so the darts "take off" partway along. Old stories claim that, in ancient times, snow-snake darts launched from ramps could fly up to a kilometer (about half a mile).

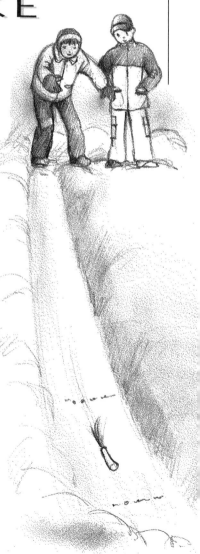

NARWHAL STRIKE

For some time, scientists puzzled over the purpose of circular stone rings on the arctic tundra. Each ring is about 1 m (3 ft.) across and is placed inside a slightly longer, oval ring. Following a discussion with Native elders, scientists concluded that these rings represent kayaks and form the play area of an ancient game for two players. One player walked around the outer oval ring dragging a strip of animal hide or rope. The other player would sit in the inner ring with a stick and, without moving from the circle, try to strike the rope on the ground as it passed. This is the kind of move a skilled hunter would make, sitting in his kayak, trying to spear a seal or a narwhal in the sea.

You can try this game with a friend using a ring of snowballs to outline the round kayak seat and a larger oval ring of snowballs to show the outline of the kayak itself. One player drags a rope while the seated player tries to touch the moving rope with a blunt stick, such as a hockey stick.

149

MAKE A RINK

Construct your own ice rink for skating, sliding and game playing — until the spring thaw.

1.

With an adult's help, decide where to locate the rink. Remove all hazards such as rocks. Pile snow, straw or used tires around trees and other immovable objects.

2.

Shovel snow onto the rink area and stamp it down with your boots. When the weather forecast predicts temperatures will stay below freezing for several days, soak the prepared rink area using a garden hose or a sprinkler. Repeat for several days in a row until the ice is at least 2 cm (³/₄ in.) thick. Do not walk on the rink while it's under construction.

3.

Once the rink is ready, keep it shoveled and use a hose to flood any cracks that appear now or later when the ice chips.

Note: Hoses and outdoor taps can freeze and burst in cold weather. After flooding the rink, turn off the tap and drain the hose completely. Ask an adult if there is an indoor turn-off valve that should be opened and closed with each use.

SKATING THREESOME

With two friends, test the new rink with this game.

- Three skaters hold hands and begin skating together in one line. The middle skater plants his skates by digging in the inside edges and swings the two outside skaters forward.

- When they are at arm's length, they plant their skates and pull the middle skater up and past them to arm's length.

- He plants his skates and swings the outside skaters forward again. Keep going as long as possible.

ICE SAFETY

Skating on ponds, lakes and rivers is a fun part of winter, but if someone falls through the ice, there are only minutes to react. Always ask an adult to make sure the ice is safe. If you're not sure, don't go onto the ice.

RINK GAMES

The games begin as soon as the ice is ready (see page 150). Strap on the blades, drop the puck and start with a game of shinny.

SHINNY

1.

Set up a 2 m (6½ ft.) wide goal at each end of the rink. Use snow boots or milk jugs filled with water as goal posts.

2.

Each player needs skates or warm boots with good treads and a hockey stick. Divide into two evenly skilled teams of three to eight players each.

3.

Teams choose a goalie and one or two players to play defense. The rest are forwards.

4.

Place the puck or ball on the ice in the center of the rink. The game begins with a face-off between one player from each team. These two players say together, "one, two, three, game on" and try to gain possession of the puck.

5.

Players try to shoot the puck past the goalie of the opposite team. Each goal counts as one point.

HOG

When there are not enough players to divide into shinny teams, try a game of hog. The object of the game is to prevent the others from scoring, while scoring the most points yourself. Whoever hogs the puck the most usually wins.

KEEP-AWAY

Played with two players, you try to keep the puck away from your opponent as long as possible. This requires skillful stick-handling and fancy skating.

RINK BOWLING

1.
Fill the bottom of 10 large pop bottles with about 5 cm (2 in.) of sand or gravel. Tighten the lids.

2.
For bowling balls, you'll need two empty soup or coffee cans for each player. Fill them with water and set outside to freeze.

3.
The bowling "alley" can be up to 18 m (60 ft.) long. Mark a start line at one end of the rink using drink crystals.

4.
Set up a triangle of 10 bowling pin bottles at the other end.

5.
For each turn, players take two throws. Clear away fallen bottles between throws. The player with the most points after 10 turns is the winner.

KEEPING SCORE

- 1 point is scored for each bottle knocked down.

- 10 bottles knocked down with the first ball (a strike) = 10 points.

- Reset the bottles, throw the second ball and score 1 point for each additional bottle knocked down up to 10 points — 20 points in total.

- Some bottles knocked down with the first ball and the remainder with the second ball (a spare) = 10 points in total.

153

ICE AND SNOW ART

If you like making sand castles in the summer, you'll love ice sculpting. Plan this activity for when the weather is below freezing.

ICE CASTLES

1.

With an adult's permission, collect as many containers as possible, including loaf, cake and muffin tins; yogurt, ice cream and margarine tubs; large and small pails; ice-cube trays and plastic cups. Spread the containers on a flat area, outdoors.

2.

Use a watering can to fill the containers. Allow to freeze overnight or until solid.

3.

Remove the ice shapes from their molds by squeezing the outside of the containers, inverting and tapping the bottom. Use a little snow to glue the shapes together. Letting your imagination guide you, decide what to make. It could be something wild and crazy or a standard castle.

4.

For a glistening finish, sprinkle lightly with water. You can color the water with drink crystals or food coloring.

MAKE YOUR OWN SCULPTING SNOW

If nature won't cooperate, it is possible to manufacture a block of sculpting snow.

You'll need:
a shovel
a watering can
a garden trowel
waterproof boots

1.

Make a small mound of snow, sprinkle with water and pat with the back of the shovel. Add more snow and repeat this process until you have a large block of icy snow.

2.

Using a garden trowel, scoop or carve away some snow, leaving behind the desired shape. You can transform the snow into works of art. Feature the creatures whose fur or feathers change color in winter to adapt to their surroundings — the arctic fox, the snowshoe hare or the white-tailed rabbit, least weasel, snowy owl and ptarmigan. Sprinkle the final product with water.

SNOW ANGELS

Made any snow angels lately? Why not try a chain of angels? You can do this by yourself or with a bunch of friends.

155

WINTER OLYMPICS

Make the Olympics happen every winter — a special event shared with family and friends. You can count on rosy cheeks, tingling toes and a day of extraordinary fun.

PLANNING AHEAD

- Form a small planning committee with an adult helper.

- Set a date, with an alternate storm date.

- If possible, pick a site that includes a small hill, a flat snowy field or lawn and a place to skate.

- Decide on the number of participants and deliver notices to your neighbors and friends.

- Invite two or more people to act as judges. They'll need stopwatches.

- Make a trophy for the winning team and the runners-up that can be used each year. Make or buy funny prizes for the other participants.

- Set up a "refueling booth" with hot chocolate and snacks.

CHOOSING TEAMS

Avoid hurt feelings on the big day by dividing the group ahead of time into two fair teams with two team leaders. Make sure each team has members from all age groups.

Using two different colors of felt, make badges or ribbons for all members of each team. Name your team after your family or favorite animal, such as the Wolverines versus the Grizzlies. When the teams assemble on Olympic Day, team leaders welcome each player and pin badges on their jackets.

CHOOSING EVENTS

Olympic Day should include group events for people of all ages as well as individual challenges. For each hour of competition, you'll need three or more events. Decide ahead of time how points will be scored and recorded. Try the following suggestions, make up your own wacky additions to the fun and check out other possibilities from this book:

Snow soccer, page 146;
Snow snake, page 148;
Rink games, page 152.

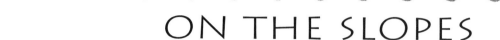

ON THE SLOPES

Who can toboggan or ski down the hill the fastest? If that's too ordinary, try some of these zany team challenges and dream up your own, too. Before the games begin, make sure an adult checks the hill for rocks and other hazards hiding in the snow. Wear a helmet on steep slopes.

ROLL RACE

Toss a coin to see which team goes first. At the top of the hill, five members from the first team lie down in a line holding onto the ankles of the next person. Record how long it takes for them to roll to the bottom of the hill. Then time the second team. The fastest team wins.

TOBOGGAN RACE

At the top of the hill, teams are given identical cardboard boxes. The judge says "go!" and each team quickly designs and makes a toboggan. The player on each team whose birthday is closest to Olympic Day slides down the hill and runs the toboggan back up to the next player. All team members must slide down the path made by the first player. The team that finishes first wins.

LUGE RUN

If the snow and temperature conditions are right, the grooves made by the cardboard toboggans will become icy, just like an Olympic luge run. With an adult supervising, try sliding down the run on your bottom.

WACKY RELAY

Teams choose four members. Two go to the top of the hill, two to the bottom. Beginning at the bottom, one player from each team runs backward up the hill singing loudly and high-fives a waiting teammate. She sits on her bottom and, making a rowing motion with her arms, propels herself down the hill. High-fives again. The third player hops on one foot up the hill, clapping his hands. High-fives again. The last player somersaults down to finish. Which team came first? High-fives all round.

SNOWY RELAY

Gather both teams at the top of the hill, each equipped with a small pail. When the judge says "go," the first member of each team takes the pail, runs to the bottom of the hill, fills it with snow, runs back uphill and dumps out the pail of snow. Continue until all members of the teams have had a turn. The judge decides which team has the biggest pile of snow. Now see which team can make the biggest snowman.

MORE

BULKY JUMPING

The long jump or hop-step-jump are a breeze in shorts and a T-shirt, right? See how far you can jump wearing your own outerwear plus the biggest adult snowsuit, mitts and boots available.

- Each team has five participants for each jump.

- Take turns jumping wearing the extra clothing.

- The judge records the jump lengths and determines the winning team.

RUNNING RACES

Running through snow can be difficult and hilarious at the same time. Using the following instructions, try these races: straight running, three-legged, wheelbarrow and running backward. Whew!

- Set up a snowy running track about 50 m (150 ft.) in length. Make a start and finish line with a string strung between two ski poles or hockey sticks stuck in the snow.

- Run the races in heats with different age groups — such as 4 to 7, 8 to 11, 12 to 16, 17 to 20, 21 and over.

- One judge starts the races and the other decides the winners.

CHALLENGES ON ICE

Make clearing the ice part of the games. Divide the ice surface in half. Provide each team with one shovel and see which team can clear its half the fastest.

SPEED SKATING RELAY

With one arm behind his back and the other arm swinging in a steady rhythm, the skater swoops around the circuit at breathtaking speed. Is it the bathing cap that makes him skate so fast? You'll need two bathing caps, four boots and an equal number of players from each team for this event.

- Place a boot 2 m (6½ ft.) from each corner of the rink.

- Players line up behind their team leader. Leaders put on bathing caps.

- The judge says "go." Staying outside the boot markers, one player from each team skates once around the rink and passes the bathing cap on to his waiting teammate.

- Continue until all members of the teams have had a turn. The winning team finishes first.

CLOSING CEREMONIES

Add up the points from each event to find a winning team. The team leaders make speeches and give out prizes. Make sure all participants are included. Award a crazy prize to the Olympian who:

- drank the most hot chocolate

- had the reddest nose

- made everyone laugh

- had the most snow in her boots

SNOW STRUCTURES

Take on a winter construction challenge — you won't need a hard hat when you're building with mini-marshmallows and toothpicks.

✳ ✳

SNOWFLAKES

Every snowflake is slightly different, depending on the conditions under which it formed and fell. But all snowflakes have six points.
To make a classic snowflake structure:

1.
Start with one marshmallow. Poke six toothpicks into the marshmallow to look like spokes.

2.
Poke a marshmallow onto the end of each toothpick.

3.
Connect the six marshmallows in a circle with toothpicks.

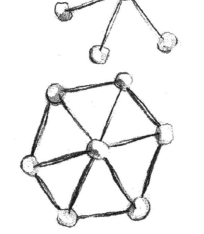

4.
Poke a toothpick into each of the marshmallows in the circle, pointing away from the center, and tip the toothpick ends with marshmallows.

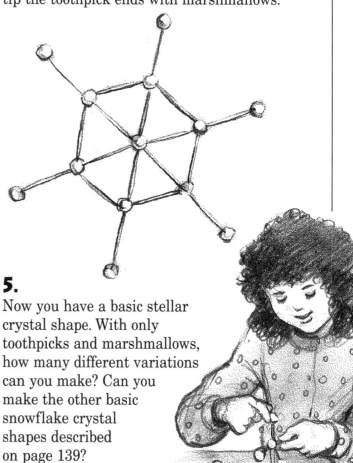

5.
Now you have a basic stellar crystal shape. With only toothpicks and marshmallows, how many different variations can you make? Can you make the other basic snowflake crystal shapes described on page 139?

MALLOW DOMES

1.

Make a triangle with three toothpicks. Hold the shape by poking the toothpicks into marshmallows at the three points of the triangle.

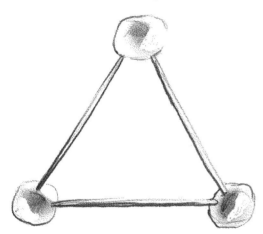

2.

Add three more toothpick and marshmallow triangles, each sharing one side with the original triangle as shown. With 10 triangles connected this way, you can form a dome.

3.

Now, challenge yourself to make a dome that starts with one five-sided toothpick and marshmallow figure, or pentagon. Add five more pentagons, each sharing one side with your first pentagon. Keep adding pentagons until you have made a dome.

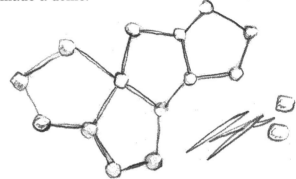

4.

The final challenge — construct a dome with six-sided marshmallow and toothpick figures, or hexagons.

CHARMS AND CHIMES

ICE CHARMS

On cold, clear days, sunlight sparkles off ice. Bring that sparkle close to home by hanging pretty ice charms outside your windows.

You'll need:
several shallow pie plates or baking pans of assorted shapes
1 m (3 ft.) lengths of colorful yarn
thin slices of orange, lemon or lime
small evergreen branches
wild winter berries

1.
Fill each pan with water to just below the rim.

2.
Circle the inside of each pan with a length of yarn so the yarn gets wet and sinks. Drape the ends of the yarn over the rim and out of the water.

3.
Place fruit slices, greenery and berries in the water inside the yarn circle. Put only a few items in each pan — the clear, empty spaces make the sparkle effect.

4.
When it's below freezing, put the pans outside on a flat surface.

5.
When solid, work the ice charms out of the pans and hang them by the yarn ends on tree branches outside your window. When your ice charms start to melt, birds and animals will eat up the fruit and berries.

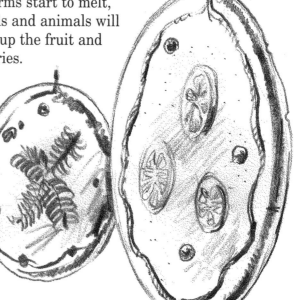

WIND CHIMES

Sometimes you can collect driftwood and shells in winter along the shore of an ocean or a big lake. Do some beachcombing to collect pieces to make wind chimes.

You'll need:

a circle of wood about 0.5 cm (1/4 in.) thick and 10 cm (4 in.) across
a hand drill and small bit
string
scissors
white glue
driftwood pieces and light shells, 5 to 8 cm (2 to 3 in.) long

1.
Ask an adult to help you drill nine small holes around the wood circle.

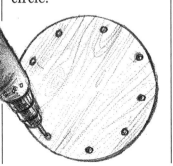

2.
Tie a piece of string 30 cm (1 ft.) long into every third hole. Tie the free end of these strings all together in a double knot. You'll hang the finished product from this knot.

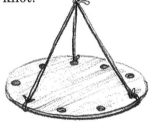

3.
The other six holes are for hanging your chime pieces. Attach strings that dangle down from these holes. The strings don't need to be the same length.

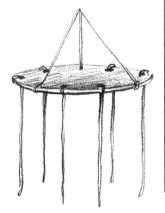

4.
Tie or glue on driftwood and shells to the chime strings.

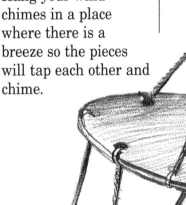

5.
Hang your wind chimes in a place where there is a breeze so the pieces will tap each other and chime.

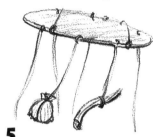

165

BLIZZARDS AND ICICLES

Bring the wildest winter weather indoors, even if there are no flurries in the forecast. Shake up a blizzard with a snow dome and hang icicles from the window.

SNOW DOME

Use a single ornament or make a frosty scene inside your snow dome.

You'll need:
a clean, small jar with a tight-fitting lid (a baby food jar works well)
a seasonal ornament or plastic figurine
waterproof glue
a glass measuring cup or jug
glitter or tiny pieces of aluminum foil

1.
Using a generous amount of glue, stick the ornament to the middle of the inside of the jar lid, leaving space to screw the lid onto the jar. Allow the glue to dry thoroughly.

2.
Completely cover the bottom of the jar with a layer of glitter or bits of aluminum foil.

3.
Fill the glass measuring cup with water and allow the water to sit until it is clear. Slowly fill the jar with water.

4.
Screw the lid onto the jar and tighten. Turn the jar lid-side down and run a bead of glue between the lid and the glass. Allow the glue to dry for several hours.

5.
Shake the dome and watch the snow flurries swirl around the ornament.

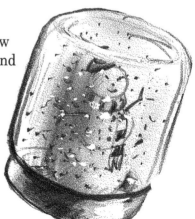

ICICLES INDOORS

Hang these crystal icicles inside a window frame and send sun sparkles through your home.

You'll need:

a paper clip
30 cm (1 ft.) yarn
a pencil
a tall, clean jar
borax (a natural laundry and cleaning product)
a long-handled spoon or stir stick

1.

Attach a paper clip to one end of the yarn and tie the other end around a pencil.

2.

Fill the jar with hot water. For every cup of water, add 50 mL (1/4 c.) of borax. Stir to dissolve as much of the borax as possible.

3.

Place the pencil across the mouth of the jar so one end of the yarn dangles down into the solution but the paper clip does not quite touch the bottom.

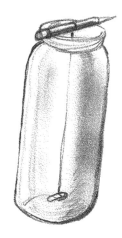

4.

Leave undisturbed for 24 hours. Pull the crystal-covered yarn out of the solution and hang to dry. Remove the paper clip. Display your crystal icicle in a sunny window.

STRING SNOWFLAKES

Make string snowflakes and hang them from a tree or place them around the plastic socket of festive winter lights. Tie them to a branch to make a mobile.

You'll need:
white pipe cleaners
white kitchen string
scissors
hairspray (CFC-free) or spray starch
newsprint
glitter (optional)

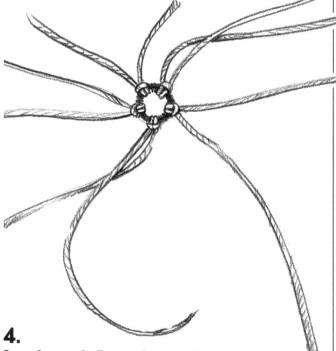

1.

Cut a 5 cm (2 in.) piece of pipe cleaner. Form it into a ring and twist the ends together.

3.

Place the looped end of one string under the pipe cleaner ring. Pull the loose ends of the string through the loop and tighten around the ring. Attach the remaining four strings evenly around the ring.

2.

Cut five 30 cm. (12 in.) pieces of string and fold each in half.

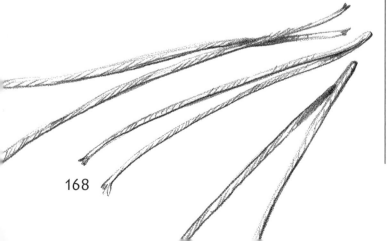

4.

Lay the work flat and separate the strings.

5.

Create a pattern of knots using a square, or reef, knot. Start with two strings side by side that originate from different looped strings. Working near the ring, pick up the left-hand string. Pass it over the right string, back under and over the top again. The end of the left-hand string is now on the right of the work.

6.

Pick up the end of the original right-hand string (now on the left) and place it over, under and over the original left-hand string close to the ring. Gently pull the two ends and tighten the knot about 1.5 cm (⁵/₈ in.) from the ring.

7.

Repeat steps 5 and 6 until there are five knots 1.5 cm (⁵/₈ in.) from the ring. Make five more knots 1.5 cm (⁵/₈ in.) away from the first set of knots. Finish with five knots 1.5 cm (⁵/₈ in.) from the second set of knots.

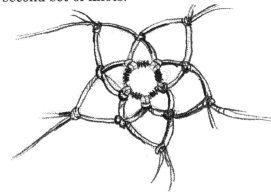

8.

Trim the excess string 1 cm (¹/₂ in.) from the last knots. Fray the ends of the strings.

9.

Place the completed snowflake on a piece of newsprint and spray thoroughly with hairspray. Dust some snowflakes with glitter while wet with hairspray, if desired. Allow to dry.

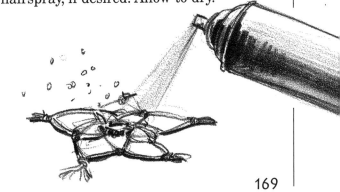

WHAT TO LOOK FOR IN THE WINTER SKY

Winter boasts more brilliant stars than any other season of the year. Look for star-studded Orion, the Hunter, and he will help you track down and name the constellations of the winter sky.

Turn the map so the direction you are facing is at the bottom.

ORION, THE HUNTER

Face south and look up. You'll see three stars close together in a row. These stars make up Orion's belt. Then look for the bright stars at his shoulders (red giant Betelgeuse and hot blue Bellatrix) and his one knee (white Rigel). Hanging from his belt is a three-star sword, one star of which is actually a nebula. On clear nights, look for the three stars that make up Orion's tiny head. Look also for the arcs of stars that form his club and shield (see story page 174–175).

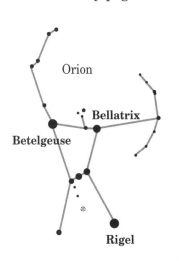

Orion

Bellatrix

Betelgeuse

Rigel

PROCYON

Follow a line east from Orion's shoulders to find Procyon, the main star in the constellation Canis Minor, the Little Dog.

Procyon

Canis Minor

ALDEBARAN

Follow a line from Orion's belt to the northwest and find Aldebaran, the yellow eye of Taurus, the Bull. A V of stars, with Aldebaran at the end of one arm, outlines the bull's face. The V is an open star cluster called the Hyades, best viewed with binoculars.

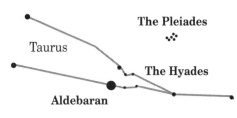

The Pleiades

Taurus

The Hyades

Aldebaran

THE PLEIADES

West of Aldebaran is a brilliant star cluster called the Pleiades. Six hot blue stars are easily seen with the naked eye, but you can see more than 400 with a large telescope.

SIRIUS

Follow a line from Orion's belt to the southeast to the brightest star in the winter sky. Sirius is the collar of Canis Major, the Great Dog.

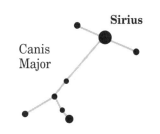

Sirius

Canis Major

CASTOR AND POLLUX

Northeast of Orion, look for these bright stars that pinpoint the heads of Gemini, the Twins. Their bodies are two lines of stars that arch toward Orion.

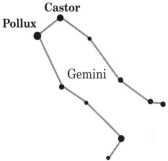

Castor

Pollux

Gemini

CAPELLA

Close to overhead on a midwinter evening, look for dazzling golden Capella, the main star in Auriga, the Charioteer. Capella sits on the edge of the Milky Way.

Capella

Auriga

INDOOR CONSTELLATIONS

When it's too cloudy or stormy outside, make your own indoor constellations so star watching can be an everyday event.

CONSTELLATION CANDLES

Yukon kids decorate these candleholders with their familiar circumpolar star patterns — the Big Dipper, Cassiopeia and Polaris — but you can choose any stars you like.

You'll need:
a clean, smooth, empty tin can
pliers
a fine-tipped permanent marker
a sharp nail
a hammer
a tealight candle

1.
Use the pliers to flatten any sharp bits around the top edge of the can.

2.
Using the marker, make a dot-to-dot of the stars or constellations of your choice on the can.

3.
Fill the can with water and freeze until solid. Remove from the freezer.

4.
Lay the can on its side on a hard surface, such as a flat rock or cutting board, and have an adult hold it firmly in place.

5.
Hammer the nail into each dot to make small holes in the can.

6.

Shake out the ice. Place the candle in the bottom of the can.

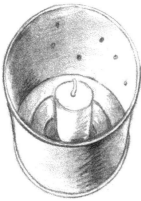

7.

Ask an adult to light the candle. Never leave a burning candle unattended.

CONSTELLATION FLASHCARDS

Test your knowledge of star names with constellation cards.

You'll need:
10 pieces of cardboard the size of playing cards
a flashlight
a pencil

1.

On each piece of cardboard, trace around the flashlight with a pencil.

2.

Using the star maps in this book, copy a constellation in each circle. Poke tiny holes through each star with a sharp pencil.

3.

Label one side of each card with the constellation's name.

ION
BIG
DIP
CASSIOPEIA

4.

In a dark room, place the flashlight on the circle and shine the light through the card onto a wall. Take turns guessing the names of the constellations.

THE STORY OF OSIRIS AND ISIS: A MURDER THRILLER

Osiris, the god of light, was Egypt's first king. Since then, the Egyptian people have connected him with the constellation Orion, the Hunter. His devoted Queen Isis has remained famous as Sirius, the Dog Star, the brightest star in the sky.

Together Osiris and his wife Isis ruled Egypt. After years of war and chaos, Osiris brought peace to the land. He was kind, clever and extremely popular. When Osiris traveled abroad, Isis stayed behind and ruled in his place. She kept a sharp eye on his jealous brother, Set, the god of darkness. Osiris trusted Set, but Isis knew he was evil.

One night when Isis was away, Osiris invited his brother and other important men for dinner. Set arrived with an exquisite box carved from Lebanese cedar, covered in jewels and gilded with gold. Set boasted that when the meal was done, whoever fit in the box could have it. The feasting went on for hours, and the box was a source of great curiosity and discussion. Various guests climbed inside, but found it too big or too small. Finally Osiris decreed that it was meant for him. The unsuspecting king got in and shouted that it was the perfect size. Peering down at him, Set laughed, slammed the lid shut and locked it. Loyal guests tried to release Osiris, but Set had his wicked henchmen carry off the box and throw it in the Nile River. When the news reached Isis, Set had already crowned himself king.

With no time for tears and her life in danger, Isis immediately began the long search for Osiris's body. She hoped her powers as a goddess could restore his life. Failing that, her husband needed a proper burial or his spirit would remain in limbo forever. Trudging from village to village along the banks of the Nile, Isis could feel their baby — the rightful heir to the Egyptian throne — moving inside her.

With the help of faithful subjects, Isis finally found the coffin. Inside, Osiris looked asleep but neither her kiss nor her magic could revive him. Grief and exhaustion were soon swept aside as her son, Horus, was born. But in Isis's distraction, the coffin was left unguarded. Set found it, cut Osiris into fourteen pieces and scattered him in the river. Isis managed to find thirteen parts and carved the fourteenth from a piece of pine. When Osiris was wrapped in linen and properly prepared for the afterlife, he rose to the sky as the constellation Orion, where he remains to this day.

The next time you look at Orion, find the three stars on his belt and then look southeast to Isis as Sirius. Can you see Osiris looking tenderly over his shoulder as they sail across the night sky?

INDEX